"Anxiety is running rampant ~~not just in our~~ in this moment in history. The Hobbses offer a down-to-earth, practical approach to overcoming anxiety that everyone can benefit from. *When Anxiety Strikes* will help you experience the breakthrough you're searching for."

MARGARET FEINBERG, author of *More Power to You*

"This book is the gift of two faithful disciples who are listening for how God is speaking through the realities and rhythms of their own lives. Dena and Jason Hobbs are prayerful theologians who offer thoughtfully integrated reflections on Scripture, brain, and body. The insights and practices they provide here promise to sustain us in difficult moments as well as reshape our responses to triggers that cannot be avoided. I look forward to sharing this resource with pastors and church leaders who want to honor and facilitate the ways many in our congregations find wholeness in our bodies and spirits."

NIKKI COLLINS, national coordinator of 1001 New Worshiping Communities, Presbyterian Church USA

"*When Anxiety Strikes* is an excellent book for anxiety management and a valuable resource within the Christian tradition. We are fortunate to have this book combining personal narrative, pastoral wisdom, and clinical insights."

HAROLD G. KOENIG, MD, director of the Center for Spirituality, Theology, and Health, Duke University Medical Center

"As a family therapist who responds weekly to persons in crisis, I am eager to recommend this practical assembly of exercises and remedies that Jason and Dena Hobbs have provided for the care and relief of those coping with these debilitating attacks. The authors write from personal experience and with spiritual insight, offering encouragement and help in the process."

DANIEL G. BAGBY, PhD, AAMFT, AAPC, Theodore F. Adams Professor Emeritus of Pastoral Care, Baptist Theological Seminary at Richmond

"The earth seems to be shifting under our feet with a global pandemic, ecological crises, wars, you name it. No wonder we are anxious. But anxiety undermines health, leads to bad decisions, and hurts relationships. And those who don't know they are anxious are actually most at risk of anxiety damaging their health or flaring out destructively. If we are human, anxiety is an issue. Saying 'have faith' is a platitude. We need real help. This book offers that help. It grounds the ancient wisdom of Scripture in our bodily experience and builds upon that scriptural foundation with practices we can actually do to make it through the week."

THE RT. REV. DAN EDWARDS, bishop of the Episcopal Diocese of Nevada (retired)

WHEN
ANXIETY
STRIKES

WHEN ANXIETY STRIKES

HELP AND HOPE FOR MANAGING YOUR STORM

JASON HOBBS & DENA HOBBS

KREGEL
PUBLICATIONS

Published by Kregel Publications, a division of Kregel Inc., 2450 Oak Industrial Dr. NE, Grand Rapids, MI 49505.

The authors and publisher are not engaged in rendering medical or psychological services, and this book is not intended as a guide to diagnose or treat medical or psychological problems. If medical, psychological, or other expert assistance is required, the reader should seek the services of a health-care provider or certified counselor.

All Scripture quotations, unless otherwise indicated, are from the New Revised Standard Version Bible, copyright © 1989 by the National Council of the Churches of Christ in the United States of America. Used by permission. All rights reserved worldwide.

Scripture quotations marked NKJV are from the New King James Version®. Copyright © 1982 by Thomas Nelson. Used by permission. All rights reserved.

Scripture quotations marked NIV are from the Holy Bible, New International Version®, NIV®. Copyright © 1973, 1978, 1984, 2011 by Biblica, Inc.™ Used by permission of Zondervan. All rights reserved worldwide. www.zondervan.com. The "NIV" and "New International Version" are trademarks registered in the United States Patent and Trademark Office by Biblica, Inc.™

Library of Congress Cataloging-in-Publication Data
Names: Douglas Hobbs, Dena, author. | Hobbs, Jason B., 1973– author.
Title: When anxiety strikes : help and hope for managing your storm / Dena Douglas Hobbs, MDiv, Jason B. Hobbs, MDiv.
Description: Grand Rapids, MI : Kregel Publications, 2020. | Includes bibliographical references.
Identifiers: LCCN 2020021715 (print) | LCCN 2020021716 (ebook)
Subjects: LCSH: Anxiety—Religious aspects—Christianity—Miscellanea.
Classification: LCC BV4908.5 .D69 2020 (print) | LCC BV4908.5 (ebook) | DDC 248.8/6—dc23
LC record available at https://lccn.loc.gov/2020021715
LC ebook record available at https://lccn.loc.gov/2020021716

ISBN 978-0-8254-4664-1, print
ISBN 978-0-8254-7701-0, epub

Printed in the United States of America
20 21 22 23 24 25 26 27 28 29 / 5 4 3 2 1

For Libby and Eli.
Our prayer is not that you won't experience difficulty
but that you know God's love and grace
in the midst of the storm.

CONTENTS

INTRODUCTION

Dena's Story

IN LATE JANUARY 1998, I lay awake for most of one night, unable to get a good breath. I was not sure if I was having an asthma attack or worse, but I knew something was *definitely* wrong. In the wee hours of the morning, I made a call to an ask-a-nurse hotline supplied by our insurance company and was referred to my local emergency room. I remember them saying that I should go to the ER because of my "deep sense of dread" regarding my condition. After my husband drove me to the hospital and helped me get checked in, I was called back to be examined. While the nurse was taking my vitals, he got a strange look on his face. My pulse was racing hard. He hooked me up to a machine that monitored my blood pressure and pulse. My blood pressure was elevated and my pulse was 120 beats per minute while I lay totally still. Within the hour a cardiologist was at my side reading my first EKG and echocardiogram. I was twenty-four years old and convinced I was about to die.

A couple of hours after I had checked in and my heart had been cleared, I was given tranquilizers to help lower my heart rate. When it calmed to below 100 beats per minute, I was discharged with a prescription for Klonopin and told to follow up with my regular doctor later that day. I am not sure if anyone uttered the words *panic attack* to me that morning.

Once home, I searched online for information about a medicine I had taken some weeks earlier for a mission trip to Africa—a once-a-week antimalarial drug, Lariam. I remembered feeling bad each week I took the pill but reasoned malaria would be worse. So despite my concerns and at the urging of my doctor and others, I kept taking the medication. But that day, as I read the responses to my online search for "Lariam side effects," tears streamed down my face. Story after story recorded how Lariam had induced panic and anxiety.

When I met with my general practitioner that afternoon, I told him I thought I was having panic attacks brought on by the Lariam. I thank God he chose to believe me. He encouraged me to make an appointment with a psychiatrist specializing in panic and anxiety and to seek supportive therapy, both of which I did.

I had no idea that day of the long road of healing that was ahead of me. I felt like I had been hit by a truck. How could this have happened to me—and why? The answers to those questions took months and even years to tease out, but healing did come. It came in layers and spirals, rising and falling, again and again, and it is still coming to me. And when it comes, it does not just heal my anxiety, but it changes my whole life. If my road had not included a struggle with panic, I cannot imagine who I would be now.

For the truth is that anxiety was a part of my life before my trip to Africa, before the Lariam, before the panic attacks. The intense panic attacks merely served as a wake-up call to an underlying condition I had suffered from so long I didn't know there was another way to live. Anxiety, like a lens through which I viewed everything, affected all of my life, but the panic awakened me. I now know how I can change that lens, keep it from controlling me, and allow it to draw me further into God's grace and healing love. Either because of nature or nurture, it is possible anxiety will always be present in my life in some form or fashion. The ongoing journey to heal my anxiety taught me and continues to teach me so much about myself, the world, and how to live in it that I cannot imagine another way. My prayer is that your journey through anxiety will draw you into healing and love as well.

Jason's Story

I am a runner. I have moved into triathlons more recently, but at heart I am a runner. Runners set a pace and stick with it. We keep going. At the time of Dena's panic attack, I was about halfway through a master of social work program at Virginia Commonwealth University. I had learned various diagnoses for mental disorders, yet despite this training, I did not know what was happening with my wife.

We had not reached our second wedding anniversary or finished our degrees. Dena still had to go through her ordination process. I still had to find a way to help house the homeless. We had set our pace and were starting our race. How could something so troubling happen after Dena's trip to Africa, a trip she had believed to be God's will for her?

After the fright of that night in the ER, we followed a trail of referrals and doctors and therapists and medications. Many of you know this trail. It starts with your general practitioner, who may prescribe an immediate-need medication like Xanax or Ativan. Then, since your anxiety disorder can affect other systems in your body, you're referred to a gastroenterologist, who checks for problems with your digestive system. You may have an endoscopy, a colonoscopy, or a gallbladder scan. You may see a cardiologist and have a stress test. And you may finally find a psychiatrist who understands the medications and how to prescribe them. And hopefully you find a pastoral counselor or therapist that "gets it."

I have to admit I did not get it at first. I was worried, frustrated, scared, and exhausted. Dena's sleepless nights were my sleepless nights too. We lived in Richmond at the time, and there were favorite places we could no longer go because she had had a panic attack there. It made no sense but anxiety is "sticky" that way. Because the terror you feel attaches itself to a place, a person, or an event, it is enormously difficult to go back to that place without reigniting that emotional state.

Most of the time I was understanding and gentle. But there were times when I was simply exhausted by it all. If you are the spouse of someone struggling with anxiety, know that it does get better. It will require patience. It will call on your endurance. Maybe that is where my running helped; I set a pace, stayed away from "the ledge," and kept going.

But I will admit that I was not always sure where God was in our struggle. In this book, we will talk frankly about the feeling that God is absent, that God has left us. If we are honest, this is how we feel at times.

There is something to be learned from the anxious periods in our lives, something God is trying to communicate to us when we are at our most frightened. Perhaps he wants us to trust him more, but anxious periods could also be a warning that something in our life is wrong. They could be our call to reach out to those around us, or they could be that proverbial last straw after a lifetime of criticism from parents, intimate others, or even our clergy.

Throughout the Gospels—in Matthew, Mark, and Luke—we read of Jesus quieting the wind and the waves in the midst of a storm. Since we see several mentions of this, we know it was important to the gospel writers. These were stormy times for the early church—they were being persecuted and killed. When the disciples ran around the deck of the boat wondering where Jesus was, afraid they were all going to drown or be struck by lightning, Jesus said, "Peace. Be still."

Dena and I have both learned to listen for that moment when God says, "Peace. Be still." Along the way we've also learned more about medication, how moving our bodies helps, how correct breathing (which seems so simple) helps so much. We have learned that reaching out to others is vital, and that our thoughts about the world affect how we feel and see ourselves and everything around us. I hope this book helps you down this path as well.

What Anxiety Is

Anxiety Is on a Spectrum

Your anxiety may be mild, moderate, or severe. Throughout Dena's life, she has experienced anxiety at different levels. If your anxiety is mild, this book and a few good friends may be all you need to discover a new quality of life. If your anxiety is further along on the spectrum, don't despair. This is in no way your personal failing, and it does not mean you have less hope. What it does mean is that you may need to ask for additional help to deal with your anxiety. Dena has found a qualified psychiatrist who prescribes her appropriate medication to help her do the work of therapy and self-care to heal her anxiety further.

While we hope that this book will be tremendously helpful to you in your journey with anxiety, *this book is not a substitute for a trained mental health provider.* If you or a loved one are unable to leave the house because of debilitating depression or anxiety, or if you or a loved one is suicidal or homicidal, please call emergency services at 911. If the need is not an emergency but it is urgent, call your doctor and discuss your symptoms.

Anxiety Is a Body-Related Event

When a clinician diagnoses an anxiety disorder, many of the symptoms are body related: racing heartbeat, tightness in the chest, chest pain (noncardiac), shortness of breath, feeling a narrowness of vision, feeling that the room is "closing in," muscle tightness, nausea, frequent diarrhea, tingling in fingers and extremities. Many people diagnosed with anxiety also suffer from physical ailments such as irritable bowel syndrome and gastroesophageal reflux disease in addition to back and shoulder pain.

Anxiety Is a Mind- and Spirit-Related Event
Throughout this book you will read about connections between the physical, mental, and spiritual. We will briefly touch on the biology of stress. There are dietary changes you can make that will help, along with relaxation techniques and breathing methods that will help you quiet yourself when you are worried or anxious. You will learn to recognize and challenge thought patterns that bring on your anxiety, and you will learn to practice soothing techniques for your body. And because we believe that we are body, mind, and spirit, we will integrate faith and community into the steps we will take together.

Our communities of faith are a tremendous resource, especially when we are hurting and scared. But cruelly, anxiety often causes us to back away from this helpful place. When we feel anxious, and certainly when having a panic attack, we can feel very alone, forsaken, fearful, and in some ways isolated from family, friends, coworkers, fellow students, and even God. One of the hallmarks of panic disorders is the sneaky way in which the fear of the next panic attack leads you to avoid places where you have had a panic attack. So you no longer go to that store or up that street or even to that church. This is why the structure of this book encourages community. We encourage you to engage or reengage those communities. Use this book in a group setting when possible.

Also, speaking of anxiety and faith, we want to include a word about our use of yoga-like exercises. We are aware that some Christians are uncomfortable practicing yoga poses as they are concerned doing so would be akin to participating in another religion. While some Eastern religions have adapted these basic and ancient postures such as standing with arms outstretched, bowing, and lying prostrate into their religious practices, these movements are simply movements and are also a part of Jewish and Christian traditions. As Susan Neal writes in her eloquent and thorough article, "Should Christians Practice Yoga?," "God knows our hearts. He knows who we are worshiping. Exercising a certain way, including yoga posturing, is not wrong or sinful because God evaluates what is in a person's heart (Mark 7:14–15, 20–23)."[1]

We have chosen to include yoga-like movements as part of our daily exercises as they so effectively reduce muscle tension and tightness while also calming the mind. Since anxiety can cause significant muscle tension and even pain, this release of body tightness is important to recovery. We have made every effort to frame the stretches we use with prayers and meditations that bring us closer to our Lord and Savior Jesus Christ, who is the ultimate healer. We hope these stretches and movements bring you physical relief and that the accompanying Christian prayers help heal your body, mind, and soul.

Anxiety Is and Is Not a Spiritual Problem

One of the more difficult questions about anxiety is whether it is a sin. Our short answer is no, sort of. Although you can find verses in the Bible that imply a yes or no, in the end Scripture is a story of our brokenness and need for redemption. With respect to anxiety, we prefer to talk in terms of brokenness because the word *sin* carries the connotation that you have done something wrong. All of us are outside of God's will in one way or another. Paul writes about that in Romans: "All have sinned and fall short of the glory of God" (3:23). There we are. All of us.

But, back to that question: Is anxiety a sin? In Philippians 4, Paul tells us, "Do not worry about anything" (v. 6). He is encouraging trust in God to provide for us. In Matthew 6, this is more artfully explained by Jesus when he says, "Do not worry about your life, what you will eat or what you will drink" (v. 25). Jesus reminds us that the birds of the air are cared for, so we will be too.

Is there brokenness present when we are anxious? Yes, broken is how we feel. Is anxiety some deliberate act of rebellion against God's will? No, we don't think so. There is a fallenness to our broken condition. Some brokenness we have chosen and some was inflicted by others. And in all of that, we pray for God's grace and healing. As we pray for healing, it will sometimes mean changing our behaviors in ways that lead to healing. And other times, that will mean forgiving ourselves and others because it is what we are called to do.

And through it all, know that God is with you. God is with us when we do not "feel" it. God is with us in our fear and worry and anxiety.

Using This Book

We have structured *When Anxiety Strikes* to be read daily for eight weeks, each week focusing on a different theme:

1. *Breath*: learning the basics of breathing techniques to soothe anxiety and stop panic
2. *Body*: learning to care for our bodies in a way that reduces anxiety
3. *Movement*: using movement such as yoga and exercise to reduce symptoms
4. *Mind*: identifying our anxious thought patterns
5. *Change*: changing patterns of behavior and thoughts that lead to anxiety
6. *Spirit*: attending to our spiritual needs and reducing spiritual shame and stigma regarding anxiety
7. *Community*: strengthening our ties with support in our family, friends, and faith communities

A final chapter, "Commissioning," guides readers through an eighth week of integrating the learning and practices into their daily lives.

While each week has its own theme, every day of the week borrows from one of the other themes. So all the daily readings in chapter 1 are primarily oriented toward *breath*, while chapter 2 primarily orients toward *body*. Yet, day 1 of *each* week includes an element of *breath*, and day 2 of *each* week includes an element of *body*. As we journey together through these days and then weeks, you will find yourself revisiting some principles and practices. The landscape may look similar, but we hope that you will find yourself looking at a particular principle or practice from a new perspective. As with the path of faith, learning to better manage anxiety is not a one-and-done accomplishment but an unfolding journey.

In addition, as you circle around to these familiar places, we hope you find that you are returning to practices, figuring out what fits best for you and your anxiety, and integrating these principles and practices into your life. In time and with practice, you will find more and more places in your life where you walk with God.

Each daily reading has a Scripture passage, a meditation or personal narrative expanding on the passage (these are most often written by Dena), a short activity, and a section with practical advice for reflection (typically written by Jason). Space on the page follows each reading so you can journal and engage with the reflections more fully. The everyday format creates a structure that can foster better habits for you. Our goal is that by the end of the eight weeks, you are more firmly on your way to recovery.

We have used this material in small group studies, and participants have reported great benefit in engaging these themes and practices in community. On the other hand, you may choose to work through this book on your own or with only one or two others. However you use the book, we encourage you to access the downloadable audio meditation prayer provided with the book's purchase.

We are so glad you've decided to take this journey of healing with us. In buying and beginning this book you have already taken your first step! There is hope and healing for anxiety. We not only believe this but have seen it countless times with our own eyes. As you learn to manage your own anxiety, know that we are praying for you and cheering you on as you return to the full abundance of life God desires for you.

CHAPTER 1

BREATH

LOSS OF BREATH

Read Ezekiel 37:1–14

*Come from the four winds, O breath, and breathe upon
these slain, that they may live. (v. 9)*

THE PICTURE WE SEE AT the beginning of this passage from Ezekiel is bleak. All signs of life for the Israelite people are gone.
There is no joy in them, no movement, no breath. All that is left
is a valley of dry bones. At times, this is what it feels like to suffer
from anxiety and panic. The fear with which we struggle can
at its worst completely take over our life. Once vibrant people
become almost unrecognizable shadows of themselves as anxiety
steals moments and days from them and the ones they love.

There are certainly times when I have felt this way. Fear over
one thing or another begins to limit my choices and activities. At
times my world has gotten small and sad. And the breath. One of
the sure signs my anxiety is flared up is that I have trouble getting
what feels like a good breath. My inhales are shallow and constricted. I hold some of my exhales back for fear that breath will
not return. Even though I fear my impending death, I am alive, but
not fully. I am not alive in the way that God wishes for me to be.

From the midst of this anxious place, consider the miracle of
Ezekiel's vision. If you read the entire passage, you may hear the
echoes of the old spiritual "Dem Bones"—one bone connected to
the other. That is the vision, bone by bone, sinew by sinew. And
after Ezekiel prophesies to the bones and sinews and the Israelites
start to look like people again, there is still one thing missing.
There is one last element that means life to a human . . . breath.
And then Ezekiel prophesies to the breath, and the breath comes

and the people rise up alive. Full life has truly returned to the people once again.

The beauty of this miracle is that breath and life can be returned to us as well. God does not wish for us to live a life of fear but instead one of fullness and joy. But how do we receive this Ezekiel-like gift of reviving breath? Our first small step in returning to fullness of life will be learning to breathe again, and the first practice we learn is that of diaphragmatic breathing. This deep belly breath triggers our parasympathetic nervous system to relax, and it reverses the effects of anxiety. It is a great tool to practice not only when you feel your anxiety rising and panic coming on, but also on a daily basis to keep your body running calmly.

We'll be exploring the practice of breath each day this week in a slightly different way. We hope that in doing so you will be able to feel God's healing Spirit blow into your brokenness, not to destroy but to rebuild. Jesus came that we might have life and have it more abundantly. This week we'll take steps to receive this gift of abundant life, one breath at a time.

Daily Exercise: Basic Belly Breath

Today you will learn how to use the muscle below your lungs that enables the breath, your diaphragm. Find a comfortable position sitting or lying down. Do this in a place and at a time when you can be uninterrupted for five to ten minutes. Bringing your focus to the diaphragm, the thin muscle that separates the abdomen from the chest, helps you take a deep, full breath. The contraction and relaxation of the diaphragm muscle is what helps us breathe. When you inhale, the diaphragm curves down, causing your belly to expand out. When you exhale, the diaphragm releases back up, and your belly falls.

To practice deep, diaphragmatic breathing, place your hand above your belly button and gradually tune into the breath. With your next inhalation, let your breath deepen to the point that your belly rises and presses out into your palm. Continue to take deeper and deeper inhalations so that your belly continues to puff out like an inflated balloon. On your exhalation release all the breath out, nice and slow. Allow the next inhalation to naturally fill your lungs deeply again. Practice this belly breathing for five minutes. As you breathe, allow yourself to gently receive more fullness of life with each full breath. When you are finished allow your breath to return to a natural flow. Notice if your body or mind feels any different. You can repeat this breathing exercise anytime you wish or feel the need to do so.

Reflection

Take a few minutes, maybe after using the breathing exercise for today, to think about when you have felt "fully alive." Write a bit about that time or place.

What do you need to connect with again so that those feelings of dryness, of death, can become life and movement, filled with the breath of God?

_____

_____

_____

_____

_____

_____

_____

_____

_____

_____

_____

_____

_____

_____

_____

DAY 2

GIFT OF BREATH

Read Genesis 2:4–9

Then the LORD *God formed man from the dust of the ground, and breathed into his nostrils the breath of life; and the man became a living being. (v. 7)*

I LOVE THIS BEAUTIFUL PASSAGE from Genesis. In contrast to the grand, sweeping creation story in the first chapter of Genesis, Genesis 2 shows us a God who carefully and specifically creates Adam. I can imagine God sitting on the new earth, slowly shaping the first human with great love and the materials of dust, dirt, and mud! We are gritty creatures for sure. God designed us to be more than a soul floating in space or some mind on a pedestal. We are embodied creatures. Crafted from the earth itself, with fingernails to catch dirt and toenails that collect sand so that we might remember from whence we came. Bodies called "good" and blessed by God. And how does God bring this enfleshed creature to life? He breathed breath into Adam's nostrils, and Adam exhaled.

But these bodies of ours have limits, don't they? From dust we came and to dust we shall return. In the meantime, we have plenty of peculiarities and struggles with these clay-made vessels. My own body is unique and wonky, with ticklish feet, moles on its neck, and a shoulder that gets sore and achy when I carry too much. And then there is the heart that races when I am scared, the gut that wrenches in times of stress, and the hands that tremble. Not to mention the strange, unexplained tingling sensations that occur in random places when panic sets in. Anxiety is a disorder of the body as much as it is a struggle of the mind or spirit.

But God blesses even this anxiety-prone body. God blesses it and calls it good. Frustrating as it can be, my anxious body has taught me to slow down and attend to the gift of God's breath and Spirit in my life. As long as I learn to live in and work with my body, these sometimes trembling hands can serve and praise their Creator. Anxiety is only part of the dirt that reminds me where I came from and then calls me back to my Creator's lips.

Daily Exercise: Three-Part Breath Awareness

Find a comfortable sitting or lying position in a place and at a time when you will not be interrupted for a while. Let your attention drift to your breathing, and become aware of its flow. Place your hand on your belly as with the diaphragmatic breath, and allow your breathing to gradually slow and deepen. As your breath flows down to the bottom of your lungs, be aware of your belly pressing into your hand. Spend a minute or two focused on this sensation of belly breath. Next, move one hand over to your body's side, along your lower ribs. See if you can feel your ribs rise outward into your palm when you breathe. Feel the sensation of your breath expanding into the ribs God knit together in your good creation. Now, move one hand to your collarbone. As your breaths deepen, your collarbone will rise at the top of your inhalation. The upper body and shoulders can be a place where we hold tension. Let your upper body and shoulders relax on each exhalation. Feel the sensation of your chest smoothly rising and falling with your slow, steady breaths. Finally, let your attention move to your back. If you are sitting in a chair or lying down, notice how your back presses into the support behind you when you inhale and releases when you exhale. Again, if you are holding any obvious tension in the back, softly let it release on your exhales. Take one more minute to feel the sensation of your upper body receiving God's gift of breath: the belly, the chest, your sides, and back. Let this breath bless and heal your mind, body, and soul. Let your body return to a normal, easy inhale and exhale. Notice any differences in body, mind, or spirit since you began the exercise.

Reflection

Dena writes about her physical experience with anxiety. What symptoms let you know you are starting to feel anxious? Part of learning coping skills is recognizing the beginnings of the anxiety. Contrary to how we sometimes feel, anxiety does not happen all of a sudden. Typically there are small signs before a full panic attack occurs. Take a minute to think about and write down your small signs.

_____

_____

_____

_____

_____

_____

_____

_____

_____

_____

_____

_____

_____

_____

_____

_____

_____

_____

_____

As you think about these signs, know that God blesses them, even in the areas in your life that feel broken. Part of knowing God's grace and forgiveness in our lives is allowing grace and forgiveness into our broken places.

DAY 3

EMBRACING MOVEMENT

Read Psalm 23

*Though I walk through the valley of the shadow of death,
I will fear no evil; for You are with me. (v. 4 NKJV)*

AT ITS VERY WORST, ANXIETY expresses itself as a fear of death. Panic attacks are such real, powerful events that the sufferer actually feels they are in danger of dying. Pain in the chest and the pounding of the heart can make us think we are having a heart attack, no matter our age or health.

When our anxiety is not expressing itself in a fear of death, there is the fear of life. *If I go to that store again, will I have another panic attack? What if I get sick on our vacation—maybe we'd better just stay home.* Thoughts and fears like these can make life smaller and smaller until there is little "safe" space left. Untreated panic disorder can lead to agoraphobia, which begins when the sense of panic becomes so large and the fear of having the next panic attack so strong that no place feels safe, except possibly home.

Once we become stuck at home as a result of our fear, we become just that . . . *stuck.* We are not traveling, walking, dancing, or moving in any significant way. If you have experienced this as I have, you know how it can steal your joy. As human beings, we were designed for movement. Look at your legs and roll your shoulders. This body was meant to get out and move!

In the beloved Twenty-Third Psalm, our lives with God are beautifully described with the metaphor of a shepherd with his sheep. Notice how much the sheep in this passage are moving. The shepherd leads them to green pastures, then to watering holes, along good paths, and even through dark valleys. The sheep and shepherd move through life together. This is precisely what God desires for you and me. God wants to lead us to good and beautiful places, if only we can get unstuck. Sure, valleys can sometimes be dangerous, and the danger can be frightening. Going through difficult places may feel like more than we can handle. But getting yourself moving does not have to start with the hard things—like taking a plane ride, driving on the freeway, or visiting that relative you have been avoiding.

Today we will start with small movements. Once our joints loosen up and our breath deepens, we can see where we will go from there. We were not meant to live in fear. If that is where you are presently, then know this is not where you have to stay. With God by our side, we can begin to move through life again. Life can be scary, but there is so much goodness and beauty as well. Today we take a step toward enjoying life again.

Daily Exercise: Gentle Walk with Breath Awareness

Find time in your day to take a gentle walk for ten to fifteen minutes. It can be at any time, in any place, and with anyone that makes you feel comfortable. If you are having a hard time getting motivated, remember research indicates that fifteen minutes of cardiovascular exercise a day can be as effective as antidepressant medication for helping mild to moderate depression and anxiety.[2] A small walk is a powerful thing! As you walk, notice the rhythm of your breathing. How many times do you inhale and exhale between each footstep? Notice your arms swinging as you move. Notice the feel of your gait. Is it long or short? There is no right or wrong answer. Notice the feeling of your steps, the surface under your feet. Be aware of how it feels to move and breathe. Even if you feel stiff, sluggish, or tired, try to be grateful that your body is indeed moving you forward.

Anxiety can lead us to draw inward, to feel small and weak and stuck. Stretching our legs on a walk reminds us that God wants us to move through those green pastures, by the cool waters, enjoying the faster pace of our hearts and our breathing. As you open your eyes to the sights on your walk, you may also notice your thoughts opening and broadening too.

Reflection

Even though we recommend ten to fifteen minutes for a walk or other exercise, remember to do what *you are comfortable doing.* Just because you do not walk for fifteen minutes does not mean you have failed. Anxiety typically forces us into an all-or-nothing thinking pattern. We feel as if everything must be "just right" or perfect. If it is not perfect, then we should not do it at all. This kind of thinking can be a barrier as we work through this book together. Your journey to healing is about small, imperfect steps.

Although we have focused on walking, what other movement-based activities could you do?

_____

_____

_____

_____

_____

_____

_____

_____

_____

_____

_____

_____

_____

_____

_____

_____

_____

_____

_____

DAY 4

WATCHING THE WINDS

Read John 3:1–10

The wind blows where it chooses, and you hear the sound of it, but you do not know where it comes from or where it goes. So it is with everyone who is born of the Spirit. (v. 8)

IN THIS CONVERSATION WITH NICODEMUS, Jesus portrays the wind as a mysterious force that comes from an unidentifiable place, blows around for a bit, and then leaves just as mysteriously. Perhaps you have had occasion to watch the wind blow. Where we live in the southeastern United States, we often see the wind kick up right before a thunderstorm. We do not so much notice the wind itself, but we see the leaves rustling on the ground, dust kicking up, and trees swaying. But if we are not paying attention, we can miss the presence of the wind altogether, even though it is always around us.

Though Jesus in this conversation is using the wind as a metaphor for the mysterious, life-giving wind of the Spirit, there are other winds that blow through our lives. In Ephesians 4:14 Paul uses the imagery of wind to describe the confusion that can result from unhelpful thinking. These winds can scatter our thoughts and unsettle our balance. Often we do not pay attention to our thoughts while they blow unnoticed through our mind like background noise. We may not notice where they are coming from, yet they are affecting us all the time. It may only be when our thoughts kick up storms of panic and anxiety that we really notice them at all.

The first step in understanding and controlling our thoughts is to pay close attention to them. Just as you can look for that small breeze in the tops of trees or the gentle movement of a flag, you can learn to notice and listen to your thoughts. Become a wind watcher—watch how your thoughts blow, how they ruffle you, what it is like when your thinking kicks up a storm within you. Like Nicodemus, we do not have to understand it all or take any action just yet. That will come in time. For now, we will practice curiosity toward what our thoughts have to show us.

Daily Exercise: Counted Breath

Find a comfortable seated position. Allow your breath to deepen as with belly breathing. On your next inhalation slowly count to five. After five beats of inhalation, let your body exhale to a count of five. If this breath is too shallow or too deep for you, you can count to a higher or lower number as it suits you. This method of counted breath is great for increasing lung capacity and for steadying the thoughts and mind.

Today we will add to this practice of counted breath a practice of thought awareness. On the inhalation, notice and acknowledge the thoughts you are having, whatever they may be. Do not judge them or be angry at yourself for having these thoughts. Just notice them. On the exhalation of your breath, release the thought and let your attention to it flow away with your breath. Again, we are not judging our thoughts or even trying to stop them or change them. We are practicing an awareness of our thoughts. Continue this counted breath/thought awareness practice for five minutes. When you are ready to finish, release the mental exercise first, and then after your next counted exhalation, allow your breathing to return to normal. Take stock of your body, mind, and spirit. Both this breathing and the ability to acknowledge and release your thoughts are there for you when you need them.

Reflection

A trap into which we sometimes fall is that of being angry or upset by our thoughts. This is particularly common in people with obsessive-compulsive disorder. In that situation, there may be a particularly offensive or frightening thought. A person's reaction of intense fear or anger to that thought actually helps make it stronger. It is better to acknowledge the thought, then gently move to another one. One neuroscientist, David Eagleman, describes our consciousness as a churning sea from which we sometimes have thoughts break through to the surface.[3] Offensive or frightening thoughts that break through should be allowed to slip like a sea monster back beneath the water.

You might also imagine a difficult thought being like a toddler vying for your attention. Sometimes it is best to say gently, "Yes, I see you," then move back to what you were doing before the interruption. Giving negative attention to the interruption can sometimes feed an undesirable behavior. You could also imagine yourself at a gathering where there is someone that you do not want to see. You might glance over a shoulder and see them, gently nod your head, then go back to the conversation in front of you. Don't give the difficult thought any more energy than it deserves.

What did you notice about your thoughts during the exercise? You do not have to write down the particulars if you do not wish to. In general, are your thoughts about certain people, situations, or concerns?

_____

_____

_____

_____

_____

_____

_____

_____

_____

_____

_____

_____

_____

WINDS OF CHANGE

Read Isaiah 43:18–19

I am about to do a new thing; now it springs forth, do you not perceive it? (v. 19)

THIS PROPHECY OF ISAIAH WAS written to God's people in Babylonian exile. Their homes had been warred upon and destroyed. Those in exile had been taken as prisoners across the desert to a strange land. Knowing they could not return home, they were bereft. Sadness and anger became a habit for them. All they knew was how to mourn.

It was to these downcast people that God introduced the idea that things were about to change. God begins to show the people the possibility they could go home. There was much rebuilding to be done. Though home was going to be different than the memories to which they had been clinging, there was new hope for their future, where formerly there had been no hope at all.

Sometimes in our journey with anxiety and panic we get familiar with being scared and sad. It becomes normal. The negative thoughts and feelings that have uprooted us from the life we once enjoyed are now all we know. And one quality of fear is that it builds upon itself. Fear tends to focus on the negative and the scary. Fear makes us draw into ourselves, our homes, our "safe" places.

Into these tight, dark places the breath of God comes, saying, "Do not get stuck in the past. Look, I am going to do something new." God reminds us that our lives do not always have to be this way. We do not have to be held prisoner by anxiety or our negative thoughts or difficult memories. The past can be the past; we can move forward into a better land that God has laid out for us.

Healing from anxiety will require us to do some new things. We may exercise more. We may talk about our fears more or with new people. We may learn to think in a new way. Most importantly, we will lay hold to the promise that God's Spirit is springing up a new work within us, a work that will feel as refreshing as rivers bubbling up in a desert.

We pray you will open yourself to the possibility of God doing something new in you.

Daily Exercise: Alternate Nostril Breathing

Breathing is so common and natural that we usually take it for granted. But since we are reading about doing a new thing today, we will also practice a new way of breathing. Alternate nostril breathing (ANB) can seem strange at first, but not only will it make you think about your breathing, it also has health benefits. Regular practice of ANB can reduce stress and even lower blood pressure. Also, it cleans out your sinuses! So let's get ready to try a new way of breathing.

Tune in to your breath. For this breathing technique, we will use the thumb and ring finger of your right hand. On an inhalation, close off the right nostril with your thumb and breathe through the left nostril only. When you switch to exhalation, release your thumb from the right nostril and use your ring finger to close off your left nostril. Exhale through your right nostril only. Keep your same hand position and now inhale through your right nostril. Switch your hand back, using your thumb to close the right nostril and releasing your ring finger from the left nostril so that you can exhale through it. Keep the same hand position and inhale left again, beginning a new cycle of breath. Repeat this pattern of inhale left nostril, exhale right nostril, inhale right nostril, exhale left nostril for a few minutes. It will take a minute or so to get the hang of this different way of breathing. Even though it seems odd at first, try not to strain, but instead breathe gently from side to side. Once you find your rhythm, allow yourself to open to this difference and enjoy a fresh, new breath. You can even visualize the breath drawing down and releasing from deep down within you, opening up areas for God to do a new work in you.

Reflection

Anxiety does sharpen our senses! That is what it is supposed to do. Though we might not face a charging tiger or some other deadly threat, we can become focused on worrisome situations around us. Yet, God asks us to look for the "new work" that he is doing in us and in the world. Where do you see just a glimmer of hope? Where do you see God's work springing forth in even the smallest of ways?

_____

_____

_____

_____

_____

_____

_____

_____

_____

_____

_____

_____

_____

_____

_____

_____

_____

_____

_____

_____

DAY 6

INFILLING

Read John 20:19-23

> *Jesus said to them again, "Peace be with you. As the Father has sent me, so I send you." When he had said this, he breathed on them and said to them, "Receive the Holy Spirit." (vv. 21–22)*

AT THE BEGINNING OF THIS passage the disciples have taken refuge behind locked doors because they are terrified. The One they had believed in and forsaken everything to follow had been killed. As Jesus's disciples, they may be next on the list to die. As bad as their fear and persecution must have been, I think the worst part for them must have been that Jesus was gone. They had loved him like no other, and now the void left by his absence must have created an ache in their hearts like no other ache.

But the good news of the gospel is that Jesus stepped into this fear and void—right through that locked door. "Peace be with you." If that were not enough, Jesus breathed on them and gave them the Holy Spirit, and they would never have to be without the presence of the divine again.

There have been times in my journey with anxiety that I have wondered where God was. My inability to feel his peace was not for lack of praying and drawing close to God. At times I have been ashamed of my fear and thought if I were a better Christian I would not struggle so much. But thankfully, the years, good teachers, and God's mercy have taught me differently. A popular saying admonishes that if we feel distant from God, then it must have been us that moved. I know what this is trying to communicate:

that we should always move toward God and not away. But I disagree with its premise that God does not move. Here, in John's gospel, we see a God who goes to hell and back, seeks us out, and then walks through doors just to be with us again. God certainly moves, and he does so to come after us in our fear and loneliness and to fill us with his own Spirit.

This does not mean that we will never feel scared, sad, or lonely again. But it does mean that even when we feel this way, we can rest in the truth that God is still with us. We may not feel the peace or the presence, but—felt or not—God is still with us.

Daily Exercise: Circle Breath

Find a comfortable standing or seated position. Begin by allowing your breath to deepen into a nice, even flow. Now add a simple hand motion with the breath. With arms starting at your side, raise them outward and upward on an inhalation until they are lifted above your head. Then allow your hands to touch overhead with your elbows bent. On the next exhalation, bring your touching palms down the centerline of your body until they rest in a prayer position over your heart. Breathe and move in a slow, flowing motion, continuing to circle your hands up on inhalation and then draw them in to prayer position down to your heart on exhalation. Do this for a few minutes, and then add an inner intention of opening yourself to God's infilling Spirit on the inhalations and drawing this good gift of the Holy Spirit down deep within you on the exhalations. Let yourself be open to the gift of God's healing, strengthening Spirit that is always available to you. You may or may not feel the Spirit's presence with you, but rest in the assurance that just as your breath is constantly with you, felt or not, the Spirit is as well. When you are ready to finish, close with your hands in prayer over your heart and notice any changes in your body, mind, or spirit. Return to normal breathing and movement, and know this exercise is always available for you to use when you choose.

Reflection

We talk often about going places to meet God or experience God. At times this can feel more like our effort instead of God's. Think about a time when God has come to you. It may have been in an expected place, like church or at a retreat where you were seeking God. But there are also times when we are hiding, scared, and fearful. God may come to us during those times through things such as a person, a song, a book, or even an animal. Write briefly about this time.

_____

_____

_____

_____

_____

_____

_____

_____

_____

_____

_____

_____

_____

_____

_____

_____

_____

_____

_____

_____

_____

_____

_____

_____

_____

DAY 7

COMMON BREATH

Read Acts 2:1-13

*And suddenly from heaven there came a sound like the
rush of a violent wind, and it filled the entire house where
they were sitting. . . . All of them were filled with the Holy
Spirit and began to speak in other languages, as the Spirit
gave them the ability. (vv. 2, 4)*

THIS PARTICULAR PASSAGE RECOUNTS EVENTS from the day of
Pentecost. One of the messages in this passage that we sometimes
miss is that it was a time of great unity. The Holy Spirit came *to
a group*, and his coming unified that group. Everyone could hear
and *understand* what the others were saying. This story is the
opposite of the Tower of Babel story in Genesis 11, a story of pride
and unity that had no need of God.

One vital resource anxiety steals from us is our social support.
This can happen for a variety of reasons. Maybe we are ashamed
to admit we struggle with anxiety. The stigma of anxiety prevents
us from sharing our burdens openly with others. Maybe in our
pride we want to handle it ourselves like the people at Babel. Or
maybe we are so scared and tired that it is hard to reach out any-
more. Whatever the reason, when we lose our community, we lose
an important resource for overcoming our anxiety. We become
disconnected from those around us. What is doubly sad—and
ironic—is that many of those around us in church share the same
fears and worries! If only we could reach out to them and face our
fears together.

When I was first diagnosed with panic disorder, I was so
ashamed that I told almost no one. Not my family, not my friends,

not my teachers. I thought the panic was my fault, that it meant something was wrong with me personally. But one day when I was struggling, our next-door neighbor asked me what was wrong. She asked so genuinely that I told her I had been having panic attacks. I will never forget how she looked at me with kind eyes, nodded her head, and said, "Yeah, I have had those too. They are really rough." I was so relieved someone else understood my struggle, I almost cried. This neighbor became a lifeline to me as I healed from that first round of panic disorder. She made an incredibly difficult time a little easier.

Like the disciples at Pentecost, we always need God to come to us. But we also need community, ideally a community of believers. Community offers us support and nurture, and it also provides us the needed challenges of community! This Holy Spirit wind from above is one that will unite us in authentic community where we share one another's burdens.

This day, know you are not alone in your struggle. There are others who suffer and know your pain, and there are others who may not understand but who love you and want to support you as best they can. Let's move toward reaching out to those who want to support us. Let us enjoy the gift of community.

Daily Exercise: Breath of Blessing

Find a comfortable and quiet seated position. Deepen your inhalations and lengthen your exhalations as you practice the belly breath. After several full, steady breaths, begin adding an intention of blessing. On each inhalation take in God's blessing for you, and on each exhalation send out God's blessing for someone else. On sequential exhalations, you can name individual family members and friends, members of the group with whom you may have been participating in this study, or those you may know with special need of God's nearness. However your prayer develops, be aware of the surrounding and uniting presence of God's Spirit that fills us all.

Reflection

Who are the supportive people in your life? Where are the places of community for you? If you have disengaged from them, what will it take to go back? Think of one or two people who you could trust enough to tell them, "Sometimes I am afraid." Jot down their names, holding these relationships in prayer and wondering with God if this is the time to be open with them about your fear and worry.

_____

_____

_____

_____

_____

_____

_____

_____

_____

_____

_____

_____

_____

_____

_____

_____

_____

_____

_____

_____

_____

_____

_____

CHAPTER 1 REVIEW

How was your experience with chapter 1?

Was there a reading or an exercise that particularly resonated with you or that you enjoyed?

Was there an exercise that you struggled to complete due to physical or other reasons?

Was there a reading or an exercise that you resisted or even disagreed with? (This is okay and normal.)

Were there places where you surprised yourself at how well you did or how your mood or health improved?

Were there places where you were surprised at how hard things were?

If there were places where you felt great or the study was easy, we rejoice. However, if week 1 was hard for you, don't despair. New habits are hard, and learning these new practices takes time. There is a reason we do this for several weeks. It is all about walking the path and doing the practice. Even when the practice is hard, you are making important progress. Do not expect perfection or judge yourself (especially against other participants if you are in a group meeting; everyone will struggle at some point). It is all grace, one small step at a time.

That being said, if you felt like you were hitting your head against a wall all week or that the course was almost impossible for you, it could be a sign that you need to increase your level of intervention. If you do not have a therapist yet, ask your group leader or a trusted friend for a recommendation. If you have a therapist and were hitting a wall all week, consider bringing up a conversation about medication. This does not mean you have to commit to medication, but you are willing to think about the possibility.

If you are struggling and need to seek out additional help, please do not beat yourself up. It in no way makes you a failure or a bad person. You are simply a person who is having a hard time. The best thing you can do is set yourself on a path that will help you get to a better place. There is no shame in asking for help. There is hope that you can get to a much better place.

CHAPTER 2

BODY

DAY 1

INCARNATION

Read Genesis 1 and John 1:1–18
And the Word became flesh and lived among us, and we have seen his glory, the glory as of a father's only son, full of grace and truth. (John 1:14)

WE READ IN THE CREATION story of Genesis 1 that God breathed over the dark waters of chaos to create life. First God's breath blew over the dark deep to speak light into being. Then God breathed over the chaos and ordered it a bit, creating a safe space between the waters of sea and waters of sky where life could thrive. God kept on breathing and speaking words of life to fill this safe space with land, rivers, birds, and fish. A sun was made to give light to the day and a moon to give light to the night. Stars were added just because God is that good. After five days of thoughtful, loving, good creation, God came to the big finish. And do you know what God created last? People. Yes, God made us as land creatures with amazing and peculiar bodies and minds that somehow reflect his image. And then he called us very good.

But that's not the most amazing part. Later, God chose to put himself into a peculiar body and to have this essence of God walk on earth with dirty feet and hairy toes. God with toes! The breath that once breathed light into the darkness gasped oxygen with tiny lungs and cried an infant's cry under the same stars he had made. This is incarnation. God chose to become enfleshed, embodied as a human being, so we could see his glory with our own two eyes. So we could be close to God, God came down close to us. By taking on a human body and then offering it for us, he brought grace and redemption.

I try to remember this incarnation when I am frustrated with my peculiar human body. For as we are incarnate, so is our anxiety. I get upset when my heart races and my breath gets shallow and quick. I wish I were something other than a creature with this flawed form. Then I return to the truth that I was intentionally crafted by God, who calls me good. I am blessed and honored to have a heart that beats like my Lord's did, even if mine does race from time to time. And when I listen to its rhythm, it tells me something. Its fast pace pounds out a message—maybe I have been running too hard, resting too little, or not dealing with an issue that needs to be addressed.

And my breath, shallow or full, reminds me that the same Spirit that blew across the waves at the creation of the world breathes in me. This same one holds back the waters of chaos so that I may live and thrive on this good earth.

Daily Exercise: Wave Breath

Find a comfortable seated position or, if possible, a comfortable position lying on your back. Place one hand over your belly and one hand over your chest, and begin to tune into your breath. Deepen your inhalations and lengthen your exhalations as with a belly breath. Notice how the breath rises and falls like the waves at creation. Spend a few moments sensing this steady rhythm. As your body rises and falls, trust that the Spirit is breathing over you even now. Breath in and receive the life and light and goodness that the Spirit brings; breath out and release anything you would like to let go into the Spirit's holding. Keep breathing in and receiving and exhaling while releasing for the next few minutes. Gradually allow yourself to return to a normal, steady breath. Stay for a moment more to notice and try to enjoy the sensations that the wave breath brings. As you move back into your day, remember that you can return to the wave breath whenever you wish to do so.

Reflection

Anxiety likes space. Where there is space, thoughts can rush in—especially the worried ones. When we have not heard from a loved one, when there is a gap between our expectations and reality, then we wait and watch. When we feel anxious, our thoughts turn to the worst. It has been shown that breathing, simply breathing, helps soothe that process, even physiologically. Note how the breath happens without you. You don't control whether it occurs. As you do the exercise today, consider what you are trying to control that will happen on its own, whether or not you want it to. Write down what you notice both before and after you practice the breathing exercise.

_____

_____

_____

_____

_____

_____

_____

_____

_____

_____

_____

_____

_____

_____

_____

_____

_____

WHAT'S GOOD FOR THE BODY

Read 1 Corinthians 6:12–15

"All things are lawful for me," but not all things are beneficial. (v. 12)

PAUL'S ADVICE IN 1 CORINTHIANS 6 is a response to some new Christians who rejected the limits of the Levitical codes. It is true that Jesus came to set us free from the law, but it is also true that much of the law was put in place to protect us. All the rules about unclean animals and avoiding people with leprous skin were meant to keep people healthy and well during ancient times. Although crab may be quite safe to eat today and most skin conditions are now treatable, it is still a good rule that just because you can do something, it does not necessarily mean you should. Not everything is beneficial.

But sometimes it is hard to know—and harder to avoid—the things that may not be beneficial. We live in a culture that is fast-paced and demanding. Most of us are disconnected from the early-to-bed, early-to-rise agrarian life that kept people in tune with their bodies and its physical rhythms. Many of us can get anywhere we need to go without walking, we can eat anything we want, and we can entertain ourselves as much as we please.

But it is not all beneficial to us. Not in the least.

How do we know when we are hurting ourselves? A good place to start is paying attention to your body. How does it respond to what you put into it and take out of it in a day? When I started paying attention to my body, I realized how much better it felt when I got up and swam a few mornings each week. The effect was not immediate, but a couple of weeks after starting the exercise, I noticed the absence of moodiness and irritability that can accompany anxiety. I also realized that if I gave up my morning coffee, my heart raced less. Since I like *not* having a racing heart, I have learned to make a cup of herbal tea instead.

What is good for my body may not be what is best for yours. You may be fine consuming coffee and chocolate (good for you!). For the rest of this week, we will ask you to do some experimenting. There are certain changes that have proven helpful for many people who struggle with anxiety. We list resources that go over the science in detail in the appendix of this book. Most of it has to do with the chemical interplay between the stress hormones (cortisol and adrenaline) and the feel-good hormones (dopamine, serotonin, and oxytocin). Blood sugar levels and vitamin deficiencies can play a part as well. Diet, exercise, and sleep are key components of any anxiety management plan. As a whole, these practices lower the stress hormones in your body and elevate the feel-good hormones. That is shifting the tide in the right direction!

If you often feel tired, try turning off the electronics and going to bed thirty to sixty minutes earlier a couple of nights this week. Sleep heals and is a key component in our health. Lack of it will aggravate your anxiety. If you read on a device before bed, try to use one without a lighted screen.

You will also want to try getting some moderate to easy cardiovascular exercise (such as walking) a couple of times this week. Though it may seem counterintuitive to exercise when you are tired, the end result is that you will feel more energetic. And you will sleep better too!

And though it is hard to talk about our diets, what we eat does have an effect on us. In general, high-sugar diets can unbalance our moods. Blood sugar highs and lows are no friend to the anxiety prone. Try having some protein and fruit for breakfast instead of a pastry to get a nice, stable blood sugar level at the start of your day. See what it feels like to replace one of your cups of coffee or soda with water. Small changes can make a big difference in how you feel.

Remember, these suggested changes are never intended to punish or deprive. They are meant to bring the nourishment and care that your body needs to thrive. Experiment with what feels good to your body. Discover what makes you feel healthy and well.

Daily Exercise: Food and Exercise Journal

Pay attention today to what you put into your body and how you use it. Take note of how you feel throughout the day. What change felt like it was good for your body? If you think your body is not thriving today, change a few things tomorrow and see how you feel. Don't stress over the details or judge yourself. Just tune in to what your body is saying, and try to hear the wisdom it has to share. Start a record today of what you eat and how much you move. You may notice some surprises when you record hour by hour what you do with your body and what you take into your body.

Reflection

Think back to a time when you felt more relaxed or settled. What were your habits then? What were you doing, what did you eat, and what was your lifestyle? Jot down notes and allow them to guide your current habits.

_____

_____

_____

_____

_____

_____

_____

_____

_____

_____

_____

_____

DAY 3

THE GIFT OF BODY

Read 2 Samuel 6:12–15

David danced before the LORD with all his might. (v. 14)

SOMETIMES WE FORGET THAT OUR bodies are good gifts from God. They were meant to bless us, those around us, and even God. Any teaching that the body is bad and should be punished or deprived is dangerous and wrong. Certainly the body can be treated badly or used to a bad end, but our bodies themselves are not bad or sinful. They are a gift, a tool that we choose to use for good or ill.

David is a perfect example of this truth. On one hand, he is infamous for how he used his body and the bodies of others to satisfy his own lust and greed. He took the body of a woman who was married to another man to satisfy his selfish appetite. If you read 2 Samuel 11, you will be reminded of how badly things went from there. This is the same man who had earlier used his body as an instrument of praise. When David had the ark of the covenant brought back to Jerusalem, which was itself a monumental and highly significant task, he "danced before the LORD with all his might." In one of his most holy moments, this man of praise turned not to his lyre or even to words of praise, but to his body—moving every muscle and fiber of his being to give glory and honor to God.

Recovering from anxiety involves a shift from being ashamed of, distrustful of, or just plain disconnected from our bodies to reclaiming our bodies as gifts for pleasure, joy, and praise. This shift does not happen overnight. For me, it happened during the early years of my yoga practice. When I was in my midtwenties and my therapist first suggested that I try yoga to ease panic and anxiety, I thought the breathing and relaxation techniques would be the most helpful. And they were certainly helpful. But I was surprised at how good it felt to reconnect to my body through the sensations of movement and stretch. Loosening my tight and tense places brought relief I did not know I needed. I was amazed and even proud of what my body could accomplish as I began to trust and appreciate it again.

This reconnection to a body once so broken and untrustworthy was a small miracle. What was even more profound, however, was that reconnecting with my created body helped me reconnect with the God who made it. Yoga practice became a time of prayer where my limbs and lungs uttered pleas and praises my tongue could not find words for. In the times of rest that followed, God offered healing back to me.

As we move into the small, gentle yoga flow in today's exercise, ponder your relationship with your body. If you have lost trust in or connection with it during your struggle with anxiety, consider the possibility of reclaiming the good gift of your body. As you move and breathe today, feel the goodness and strength of your body. Enjoy the pleasure of its movements. Let your body become an instrument of prayer and praise.

Daily Exercise: Half Sun Salute

Begin in a standing position with your feet slightly apart, arms at your side. Inhale as you lift your hands up over your head. On an exhalation, tilt back slightly into a standing backbend. Take a breath here with your heart open and hands uplifted to God. On your next inhalation stand upright again, arms stretched up and hands open. Then on your next exhalation roll forward as if you might touch your toes. If you have a contraindication,[4] do not lower your head past your heart; otherwise, let the crown of your head drop down. Take a breath in this bowed position. On your next inhalation, roll up and stand with your hands lifted overhead. Finish on an exhale with your hands resting over your heart in prayer position (hands folded together). Repeat the movements, adding an intention of prayer. In the upright and lifting movements, praise your Maker. In bowing movements, humble yourself before God while offering prayers of supplication. When you finish the second time, let yourself settle in standing prayer for a moment so your body can soak in the effect of your movements and prayers. You can come back to this moving prayer whenever you wish.

Reflection

Many people have heard of the fight-or-flight response of our sympathetic nervous system. When we feel threatened, we either become aggressive or we prepare to run. However, there is also a neglected third response that we can have: we freeze. Think of a possum on the roadway at night when a vehicle is barreling toward it. Freezing is a disconnection or disassociation between our bodies and our present experience. It can occur during difficult or anxiety-producing situations where we are not able to run or fight, but it sometimes happens in situations where we should remain engaged and physically present with our loved ones.

Consider ways or times when you have felt outside of your body. If these thoughts are troubling, then consider the ways you are feeling now. Jot down times when you have felt connected and present, remembering that God wants this for us—to be as fully present as David was when he danced in front of the ark.

_____

_____

_____

_____

_____

_____

_____

_____

_____

_____

_____

_____

_____

_____

_____

_____

_____

_____

_____

_____

_____

_____

_____

_____

_____

_____

_____

RECONNECTING WITH THE BODY

Read 1 Corinthians 12:12–26

But as it is, God arranged the members in the body, each one of them, as he chose. If all were a single member, where would the body be? (vv. 18–19)

PAUL WROTE THESE WORDS TO the church at Corinth because they struggled to be a unified community. Instead of acting as one body, they were quite divided. Some people did not like or did not agree with others in the church, so they removed themselves from each other. Paul uses the image of the body to explain how connected the church really is and to show that we cannot cut ourselves off from others in Christ's communion. Just as it hurts to lose any part of our body, to be "cut off" from the body that is the church hurts us too!

How ironic that I, as an anxiety sufferer, have tried to do this very thing with my physical body. My mind has said to my constricted lungs, "I do not like you. You make me feel afraid when I am not actually in danger; therefore I will disconnect from you and the discomfort you bring me." My mind has said to my trembling, tingling fingers, "I am embarrassed by you and do not trust you. You are not that important to me anyway, so I shall ignore you altogether."

To some degree this coping mechanism is necessary so I do not spend all day worrying about the strange feeling on the left side of my chest. But over time, disconnecting from our bodies can be as destructive as a church fight. We can end up like a floating head cut off from the rest of our body because we have become so mentally removed from it. This is not good for us. We need those lungs and trembly fingers to function properly. We even need to listen to their negative messages because they have something important to say.

As part of our anxiety management, we will work on reconnecting with our body, reintegrating with it. At first, we will just check in with all our different parts. Maybe it has been a while since we said hello. Maybe there needs to be some peacemaking between you and your more difficult members. Over time trust can begin to build again between you and your body, and you will be able to hear what it is saying to you.

But today we will simply say hello to all our parts.

Daily Exercise: Warm Bath or Shower

Draw yourself a nice, warm bath or take a long shower at a time when you have the space and privacy to relax. If you are taking a bath, use bubbles or candles or music or any nice add-ons to make the experience more pleasant and relaxing for you. If you are in the shower, use a nice soap or scrubby or whatever makes your shower a more sensate and pleasant experience. As you soak in the gentle waters, take time to note and connect with your whole body. Wiggle your toes. Feel the tingle of the bubbles on your fingertips. Notice how the warm water feels on your shoulders and back. Were they tense or tired? Give them permission to relax and enjoy this safe space. Massage your face and temples. Maybe even treat your hair and scalp by massaging it with warm oil (coconut oil does wonders for hair and skin!). Spend at least twenty minutes just being in your body. Be as kind to you and your body as you can. When you are finished, pay attention to how you feel. Maybe you can tune in and connect to your body again at some later time.

Reflection

Because anxiety is such a physiological, body-based event, I generally spend time talking with people about how to soothe themselves physically. We used to think that our thoughts always preceded our feelings, but more recent research shows it is more complicated than that. In one interesting experiment,[5] people forced their face into a frown by holding a pencil between their lips. Another group forced their faces into smiles by holding a pencil between their teeth. Then each group was shown a cartoon. The ones who were forced into a smile found the cartoon funny, while the group forced to frown did not. The old management strategy of answering the phone with a smile on your face so you will sound happier may just be true!

Our bodies matter. How we hold ourselves matters. How much we smile matters. Consider how to help yourself feel better physically, because in many ways the mind will follow. Write down what would feel good to you physically. Perhaps it is sitting up straighter, smiling more, or moving more. Write down something you will try to do today.

_____

_____

_____

_____

_____

_____

_____

_____

_____

_____

_____

_____

_____

DAY 5

LISTENING AND RESPONDING
TO THE BODY

Read Luke 24:13–35
*They said to each other, "Were not our hearts burning
within us while he was talking to us on the road, while he
was opening the scriptures to us?" (v. 32)*

ONE OF THE GIFTS OF the body, if we listen to it, is that it gives us
important information. If our heart and stomach flutters when we
meet someone, our body may be saying this is someone we want
to know better. If our hands sweat in a tense situation, our body
may be saying we need to speak up and offer our perspective.
Or like the disciples, maybe our body alerts us to the closeness
of the divine. The disciples' minds did not tell them they were in
the presence of Jesus while they were walking that Emmaus road,
but their burning hearts did. Perhaps like the disciples and John
Wesley, your heart has been "strangely warmed" in a moment of
worship.[6] Or perhaps like me, the hair on the back of your neck
rises when the Spirit moves. Our bodies are wise in their own way.

As frustrating as it may be, my noisy and reactive body has
given me a lot of important information over the years. Anxiety
brings change to my body systems. It changes my stomach, my
breathing, my skin. When my gut flares up with any type of dis-
tress, I know to pay attention to what is out of whack not only
with my digestion but with my life. Have I overcommitted myself
again? Am I neglecting self-care that is not a luxury but a necessary part of my life? Has a job situation or relationship changed
in a way that has become unhealthy and untenable?

Instead of viewing my body as a malfunctioning enemy, I have come to see it as a type of early warning system about what might be off in my physical and emotional health. It may be time to make a change in my life. My warning system has led me to leave hostile work situations, work on difficult relationships, and even refrain from taking medications that do not mix with my body chemistry.

In addition to listening to what makes our bodies react negatively, it is important to hear what makes our bodies hum with joy. What foods, people, and experiences make you feel alive and well? Tend these relationships, participate in these events, and make space for these moments of connection in your life.

Daily Exercise: Journaling

Take some time to sit and journal. Think back over your journey with anxiety. What are the physical signs that let you know your anxiety is flaring up? Is there a physical sign that manifests itself repeatedly? Is there an "early warning" sign for you? Spend some time remembering your story and the physical signs that have accompanied it. How does your body change under anxiety's influence? What are practices your body responds to positively? Think back on your breathing, walking, and diet changes. Note how these positive changes affect your body.

Reflection

Once we have this information, what do we do with it? One of my favorite phrases, heard early in my career, is "Insight does not equal change." Knowing we have a problem is important. Listening to the information your body gives about your anxiety and its source is important. But in the end, we have to think about change.

Much of this chapter has been about listening and reconnecting with your body, but now that you have this information, what do you do with it? Think of one small change you may have already started. Or consider one small change you may want to start. Write it down and consider how you will begin to make this change a part of the coming days and weeks and beyond. Plan for how you will make and maintain this change.

_____

_____

_____

_____

_____

_____

_____

_____

_____

_____

_____

_____

_____

_____

_____

_____

_____

_____

_____

_____

_____

_____

_____

_____

_____

_____

_____

CLAIMING THE BODY
AS SACRED

Read Psalm 139:1-18

For it was you who formed my inward parts; you knit me together in my mother's womb. I praise you, for I am fearfully and wonderfully made. (vv. 13–14)

IT IS A STRUGGLE FOR people in modern-day America to accept their bodies as good enough. Even those who are not prone to anxiety struggle with being critical of their bodies. If you do struggle with anxiety, such widespread complaints are only compounded by your specific frustrations with your body. We often are critical of our bodies for what we perceive as their inadequacies or malfunctions.

During the years we tried to conceive a child, I collected little things for our baby. One such item was a beautiful paper bookmark that said, "Angels dance for joy over you, beautiful child of God." I saved the bookmark so the child would grow up knowing how wonderful, beautiful, and loved he or she was. On one particularly anxious day when we had still not conceived, it hit me that this bookmark's statement was as true for me as it was for our future child. Yes, even my wonky, infertile, and anxious body had been wondrously and beautifully made and was a cause of joy for the angels.

If you have not accepted this truth yet, let me make it clear. God has made *you* a wondrous, beautiful, and sacred being. No matter how critical you may be of yourself, God and the angels find *you* a cause for joy. You were not a mistake or a defective creation. Rather, you were designed intentionally and specifically by the Creator of the universe. You were knit together in such a beautiful way that angels dance at your very being.

It is not always easy for us to accept this good news. We have been brainwashed to believe otherwise. Let this spiritual truth sink in. Draw close to the source of beauty that made you and loves you—just as you are.

Daily Exercise: Progressive Muscle Relaxation

For today's exercise we will be practicing a modification of a progressive muscle relaxation. We will enjoy the more traditional form of this helpful relaxation technique later, but today we will start with this twist.

Find a comfortable lying-down position, and take a few cleansing breaths. Start with your feet. Flex your feet and remind yourself that your feet were wonderfully and fearfully made, and then relax them into God's care. Then squeeze your leg muscles and bottom. Remind yourself that your legs were crafted by God's loving hand, and then relax them into God's care. Squeeze your hands and tighten your arms and shoulders. Remind yourself that your arms are sacred gifts from your Maker, and then relax them into God's care. Take a big breath of air so that your belly and chest rise. Remind yourself how your inner parts were knit together as a miracle of God, and then relax them into your God's loving care. Stretch your facial muscles long by opening your eyes and mouth wide, and then scrunch your mouth up into a tight prune face. Remind yourself that you were made with beauty by the source of all beauty. Relax your face, head, and neck into God's loving care. Scan your body for any remaining tension, and then with a cleansing breath release into God's hands the tension you are holding. If you would like, stay in this peaceful state for a few minutes. Then gradually deepen your breath and wiggle your fingers. Stretch gently as you awaken from your rest. As you move back into your day, take with you the knowledge that all your parts are blessings from God.

Reflection

Find one thing that you think is good about you physically. Maybe it is not visible, but it is internal. Write this down. Now, as you consider this one thing, remember that God sees all of you and says, "It is good."

DAY 7

OUR BODIES NEED
OTHER BODIES

Read Matthew 8:1–4

*Jesus reached out his hand and touched the man. (v. 3
NIV)*

LEPROSY IN THE ANCIENT WORLD was a horrible illness. If you
were a leper, you could never be touched in order to avoid spread-
ing the disease. Can you imagine never being touched? On any
given day I kiss my husband, cuddle my dogs repeatedly, and give
my teenagers overexuberant hugs. How much I would miss these
acts of touch! But leprosy meant more than just a lack of touch:
it meant a lack of community. Once declared a leper, a person
had to leave their home and live on the margins of society. There
would be no more family dinners, no more attending worship.
A life of isolation and loneliness was the leper's true curse. They
were separated from their community and in some sense separated from God too.

In light of this, notice that Jesus healed this leper *with a touch.*
Not only did Jesus heal the man of his physical leprosy, but he also
addressed the man's emotional need for touch and connection.
Healing meant the leper could finally return to the community!
He would be lonely no more.

Our bodies were never made to exist in isolation. We were created to connect to other people in a physical way. This is the way
we create and pass on life, but it is also the way we sustain life.
Numerous studies have shown that babies who are not touched
do not thrive and may even die.[7] There is a reason that NICUs
use touch as a therapeutic intervention to help children survive

and thrive. Good physical contact not only brings us comfort and companionship, it brings healing to our broken places.

Part of my physical brokenness is a shoulder that flares up on occasion. When this happens, I often get a therapeutic massage to ease the pain. While my therapist tends to my sore shoulder, I often think of James 5. This passage instructs us to lay hands on the sick among us and anoint them with oil (v. 14). As the therapist's oiled hands soothe my injured muscle, I understand James 5 in poignant ways. Of course our healing efforts would involve touch!

While we don't know exactly what the laying on of hands in James's writing would have looked like, we have an idea of the kind of touch that would be healing for us. Are you buoyed by the hugs of friends and family? Does holding a loved one's hand calm and soothe you? Even something as simple as petting your dog may increase the oxytocin levels in your body (and your dog's too!),[8] and along with this increase in the "bonding" hormone, there is a decrease in the stress hormone (cortisol).

Daily Exercise: Share a Safe Touch

Think about a safe and mutually positive physical connection for you and somebody else today. Maybe you can hug a friend. Maybe you can cuddle a lover or hold a child. It may be something as simple as stroking your pet or getting a massage or a pedicure. Whatever it is, allow it to bring healing to you and your body.

Reflection

What are your barriers to touch? As a social worker working with children and adults who have been physically or sexually abused, I know many of them have to slowly get accustomed to touch again. Even the touch of a friend, as in a hug, could make them wince as if in pain. Remember this the next time your church passes the peace or asks you to greet your neighbor. Not everyone is comfortable with that hug!

Think about what feels safe to you right now. Think of how you can communicate that to others. Consider those times when you want to ask for a touch or a hug. Be aware that refusing touch is always a valid response too. Write down what you need physically from the people around you.

CHAPTER 2 REVIEW

How was your experience with week 2?

Was there a particular reflection or exercise you connected with or especially enjoyed?

Was there a specific reflection or exercise that was difficult for you in some way?

Was there a time in the week where you were proud of yourself or surprised yourself in a good way?

Was there a time in the week where a difficulty caught you off guard?

If this week was hard for you, you are not alone. The body is a difficult subject for many reasons. Some people have struggled for decades with feeling overweight and disliking their physical appearance. Some struggle with eating disorders. Some of us have been physically or sexually abused. Even if you personally have never endured a physical trauma, many of us do carry trauma within our bodies.[9] There have been times when I've been getting a massage or doing yoga and sadness or anger has emerged from a place it was held in my body. Such pop-up emotions can catch us off guard. When dealing with your body, please go gently and give yourself grace. The good news is that, as you clean out the trauma, stress, and negativity from your body, a healthier you will begin to emerge.

If you have suffered a bodily trauma, whether from abuse or otherwise, and this week triggered difficulty for you, please reach out to someone who can help you process these deeper emotions. Deep healing is hard work, but in the end it is well worth it. There is hope and healing. Our relationships with our bodies can be made new.

CHAPTER 3

MOVEMENT

DAY 1

WINDS OF FREEDOM

Read Exodus 14:10–22

Then Moses stretched out his hand over the sea. The
LORD drove the sea back by a strong east wind all night,
and turned the sea into dry land; and the waters were
divided. The Israelites went into the sea on dry ground,
the waters forming a wall for them on their right and on
their left. (vv. 21–22)

THE CROSSING OF THE RED Sea is a beloved story in both Jewish and Christian traditions. We are so familiar with this story that sometimes we remember only the main points and forget the details. We probably remember that it is the story of the Israelites moving from a life of slavery into a future of freedom, but we may forget how terrified they were right before they crossed the Red Sea to secure their new identity.

Like the Israelites in Egypt, when we suffer from anxiety we are bound in a kind of slavery. We do not have the freedom we once enjoyed to move around and function fully in our lives. Panic and fear may have limited the places we go and activities in which we participate.

But God does not wish for us to be bound by fear and trapped in our own anxiety. Ours is a God who comes to set free those enslaved by any circumstance or oppressor. But there is a small catch: In order to be set free from bondage, we have to be willing to move. This is not as easy as it may seem. As awful as it is to be trapped by fear, we are often scared to move from it, afraid it may be even worse if we do.

What strikes me about the Red Sea story is how merciful God

is to the Israelites as they move. As they leave Egypt, God guides them by pillars of clouds and fire. He protects them by angels as the oppressor chases after them. And then the breath of God blows an east wind to move the sea in front of them so they could pass safely from bondage to new life.

Similarly, as we begin our movement from bondage to freedom, God will fight the great oppressor, *Fear*, for us. Even as we stand on the brink of freedom and tremble with fright, we can know the breath of God is moving in our lives. That breath is clearing a path ahead of us and creating a hedge about our way. Take courage, breathe in, and get ready to make your move.

Daily Exercise: Blowing Breath

Sometimes the movement of our own breath is the first movement with which we need to get reacquainted. Today we will practice a blowing wind, reminiscent of the wind that blew over the Red Sea to push back the water and clear a new path.

Find a comfortable place where you can pay deeper attention to the flow of your breath. Deepen your inhalations and exhalations. Once you have a nice, steady rhythm of deep breathing, focus on the exhalations. On your next exhalation, purse your lips as if you were blowing out birthday candles and blow your breath out slowly though your mouth. Take another deep inhalation, and continue this long, slow blowing exhale of breath from your lips. As you blow, think of how the breath of God is clearing a new path for you even now. As you repeat each exhalation, join with God in clearing these new ways in the wilderness. Let your breath blow away any fear that prevents you from moving into these new paths. Don't force your breath, but instead join with God in the gentle, steady exhalations that will prepare your way. After a few minutes, return to a relaxed breathing through your nose. Take a moment to soak in the new possibilities that are being created for you, even possibilities that you might not yet be able to see.

Reflection

We are again at the first day of our week, remembering breath and breathing, noting God's breath in us and the way that God's breath and wind moves all around us. As Dena noted, the barrier to our freedom is often our own familiar fear. We know what it feels like to be where we are, even if that place is scary to us, but God's wind or Spirit pulls us forward, even when such movement inspires worry and fear.

Memory is a funny thing. Looking back at our journeys with God, we are sometimes able to see the how and why of our paths. The places God brought us through, even though they were difficult. We are never told we will *not* walk through that "valley of the shadow of death" (Ps. 23:4 NKJV). Beginning this week, consider a time in your life when, although things may have been difficult or scary, there was some good that God had in store for you. Write down a few sentences about that event and the good that came from it.

_____

_____

_____

_____

_____

_____

_____

_____

_____

_____

_____

_____

_____

_____

_____

DAY 2

MOVE, DON'T FREEZE

Read 1 Kings 19:1–10

So [Elijah] got up and ate and drank. Strengthened by that food, he traveled forty days and forty nights until he reached Horeb, the mountain of God. (v. 8 NIV)

ELIJAH IS GOING THROUGH A stressful event in 1 Kings 19. He has just completed a showdown at Mount Carmel with four hundred fifty prophets of Baal. Both the prophets of the false god Baal and Elijah, the prophet of Yahweh, prepared sacrifices atop the mountain. The sacrifice that was burned by fire from heaven would show the Israelites who was the true God of the land. After much effort, the prophets of Baal came up empty. Then, in dramatic fashion, Elijah prepared a sacrifice that God mightily consumed. After the sacrifice, a long drought that had plagued the land was broken.

The shaming of her prophets and false god angered Jezebel, wife of King Ahab. She vowed to kill Elijah, and Elijah knew she would do everything in her power to fulfill this vow. Without many other options available to him, Elijah ran for his life. He headed deep into the wilderness where he lay down under a bush and prayed to die.

Elijah's actions are a fairly good portrayal of the fight, flight, or freeze response we experience in times of danger and stress. The fight, flight, and freeze responses are God's gifts to help us survive life-threatening situations. When a predator threatens—whether a tiger or a vengeful ruler—adrenaline pumps, muscles tighten, vision narrows, and bowels and bladder empty so we can run as fast as possible to save ourselves. If flight is not possible, our bodies prepare for an intense battle.

But what happens when the threat is over? Or when the threat is not severe and isolated but a strange, constant, low-grade threat? Or when the threat is not life threatening or even serious, but our body and brain react as if it is? When the body repeatedly prepares to fight or flee without actually doing either, stress hormones build up in our system and our muscles stay tense. We may need to run or bike or swim to discharge our adrenaline. We may need to stretch our overly tight body in order to bring it back to a normal state.

Movement is key to healing our bodies from the fight, flight, or freeze response. This is why activities such as cardiovascular exercise, yoga, and tai chi are such effective treatments for anxiety. Dena has found a mix of swimming, walking, and yoga to be effective in managing her anxiety. Jason prefers running, strength training, and stretching, and he often signs up for races or triathlons to be in "safe stress" environments. Whatever your magic combination is, find some enjoyable movements that help your body reclaim its calm state. Whatever you do, don't stay in the freeze response. Let your body move.

Daily Exercise: Body Scan

The body scan meditation is similar to the progressive muscle relaxation exercise but without actual movement. Body scan exercises bring awareness to tension and other sensations that we were not previously aware of. They also help us acknowledge different sensations without feeling the need to judge or change our bodies. If I am always feeling negative about my achy knee, I lose gratitude for it. But if I can accept the knee just how it is, I move to a healthier place with my body as it is today.

Find a comfortable lying-down position when you have at least ten minutes to devote to this practice. Take a few centering breaths as you get comfortable on your back. Then let your attention move to your feet. Notice any sensations in your feet without judging them as good or bad. After a moment, wiggle your toes freely, circle your feet, and then let your attention release. Next, let your attention center on your legs. Notice without judgment any sensations that may be in your legs. After a moment shuffle your legs freely, and let your attention release. Now let your attention center on your hands and arms. Notice any sensations that may be occurring in this area of your body. Take note if any of these sensations are surprising or something you weren't previously aware of. After a moment wiggle your fingers, gently shake your arms, and let your attention release. Move your center of attention to your torso. Simply observe without emotion any sensations in your hips, belly, and chest. Pay careful attention to any tension in these areas, without judging the tension. After a moment take a cleansing breath, wiggle your shoulders, and release this attention. Finally, center your attention on your head and neck. Notice any sensation in the face and throat. Again, be aware of any tension or tightness without judging the sensations. After a moment, wiggle your facial muscles, and release your attention. Spend a couple of moments just observing the sensations throughout your whole body. Then slowly wiggle your fingers and toes, and stretch in any comfortable way. Then gently transition from the body scan back into your daily routine. At any point you can come back to this nonjudgmental practice of noticing and observing the body's sensations.

Reflection

A book I talk about often is *Why Zebras Don't Get Ulcers* by Robert Sapolsky. While the title is humorous, the way the author details the effects of chronic, low-grade stress on our bodies is not at all funny. Sometimes we talk about stress as simply a mental event, but in fact, it involves every part of us—our entire body and the systems that maintain it. This is so much the case that most of us can merely think of a stressful event—such as a job loss or cancer diagnosis or heart attack—and begin to have *the same body reactions* we would if the event were actually occurring that very moment!

We need to move in order to discharge that stress, to release the effects it can have on our bodies. Consider the movement that best works for you. As we have mentioned before, studies show that cardiovascular exercise for fifteen to twenty minutes, three to four times per week, is enough to ease symptoms of mild to moderate anxiety and depression. Start small, but make a plan for what you can reasonably do today and moving forward.

———————————————————————————
———————————————————————————
———————————————————————————
———————————————————————————
———————————————————————————
———————————————————————————
———————————————————————————
———————————————————————————
———————————————————————————
———————————————————————————
———————————————————————————
———————————————————————————
———————————————————————————
———————————————————————————
———————————————————————————
———————————————————————————
———————————————————————————
———————————————————————————
———————————————————————————
———————————————————————————
———————————————————————————
———————————————————————————

BORN TO MOVE

Read Genesis 12:1–9

*And Abram journeyed on by stages toward the Negeb.
(v. 9)*

MANY OF US HAVE READ the story of Abram and Sarai being called to leave their home and move out into this new land of Canaan. What we do not often grasp when we read this passage is how much movement this story is actually describing. First, metaphorically speaking, it is a huge move to leave one's home (and homeland!) for the unknown based on a trusting relationship with God. But remember, there was no rental truck or moving service to take them to the promised land. For them and their belongings, there is a lot of physical movement involved as well! One day when I taught this story in a children's Sunday school class, I tracked Abram and Sarai's movements on the map from Haran to Canaan. I was shocked at how far they traveled—around five hundred miles! When I began to think of covering those miles on foot or on camelback, I was amazed. As modern people who can circle the globe in a matter of days, we have little sense of the endless walking and hard work that made up everyday life in the ancient world.

Such a lifestyle, however, may have been better suited to the way we are made. Human beings are creatures that were made to move. Most of us knew this intuitively as children. Arms and legs and amazing joints let us move our entire bodies through space. We did cartwheels, played tag, and jumped rope. When we grow up and stop using our bodies for such movement, we are like prized racehorses stuck in a small pasture to eat hay and swish their tails.

There is a message for us in the call of Abram and Sarai. We are not made to hole up in a safe place and hide. We are called to move out in faith with God. There is something powerful about answering the call by putting our bodies in motion. Long journeys over land and long journeys of the heart both require us to take the first steps. We must let our legs lengthen, let our arms swing out, and find our stride.

Daily Exercise: Go for a Walk

Take some time today to enjoy a nice walk. You can go with someone else or alone, whatever is best for you. If you are feeling strong today, maybe walk a little longer than you did in week 1. If you are feeling brave today, maybe take a route that is new to you. Allow yourself to feel safe enough, but throw in a little challenge as if *you* are like Abram and Sarai out on a new adventure. While you are walking, enjoy the fullness of your movements. Admire the length of your legs in their stride. Embrace the swish of your arms as they swing. Allow your breath to move fully and briskly in and out of your lungs. If you feel your heart beating, appreciate how it is moving good oxygenated blood throughout your body. Maybe you even can notice the movements around you—children at play, people walking or jogging, and even animals scurrying about. Know that this simple act of putting one foot in front of the other is a prayer of obedience. You are answering God's call to be a person on the move.

Reflection

There are really two things that you are asked to do today. One is clear: go for a walk. The other is deceptively simple: notice what happens. This is what the term "mindfulness" means. It is about being present, noticing everything around you. Sometimes we fall into the trap of focusing on a goal or destination instead of noticing the process of getting there. Having a destination is important, but so much of what God has to show us is about the journey too. The lessons we learn along the way guide our travels and may even change the destination.

For journaling, write down what you noticed on your walk. It may be something you have seen many times, but today you saw it in a different way. In a second, separate section, take note of where you are right now on your journey. What do you notice about where you have been and where you are now, in your body and in your spirit?

_____

_____

_____

_____

_____

_____

_____

_____

_____

_____

_____

_____

_____

_____

_____

_____

_____

_____

_____

_____

_____

DAY 4

STRETCHING YOUR MIND

Read Acts 11:1-18

And they praised God saying, "Then God has given even
to the Gentiles the repentance that leads to life." (v. 18)

THE JEWISH FOLLOWERS OF CHRIST who made up the early church
believed that salvation from God belonged to the chosen people.
This thought had been rooted in their minds since birth and came
down to them from the traditions of their ancestors. There was
probably never a consideration that anything could be different
than this belief that the Israelites were chosen by God and others
were not. This stringent belief created a divide between the Jews
and everyone else (Gentiles).

Into this long-held mindset came a new idea. In the previous
chapter, Acts 10, Peter had a dream about eating nonkosher food,
followed by God instructing Peter to talk with some people who
had just arrived. These people were "unclean," yet God had told
Peter to accept into the group anyone who "fears [God] and does
what is right" (v. 35). The result was that a tightly held thought
was going to need to stretch open a bit. There had been a movement of God that required a corresponding movement in the mind.

It must have been confusing—and even a bit scary—for Peter
and the early church. But they obeyed, stretching open the constricted places in their minds to allow a new idea to emerge. God
had given even the outsiders the repentance that leads to life.
Out of this new way of thinking, life and growth bloomed in the
church and in those believers. Their once tight minds became
receptive places for the Spirit to blow afresh.

Each of us also has ideas and beliefs we hold tightly in our

minds. These may be so deeply rooted that we are almost uncon-
scious of their presence. They are simply part of the way we think.
Sometimes, though, such thoughts and ideas may become unhelpful to us and impede our life and health.

There may come a time when we are asked to allow our thoughts
to stretch and even move. We may need to open our minds to new
possibilities. We may need to release some stiffness of thinking so
the Spirit can move anew in our lives. To practice this stretching
of our mind, we will pair it with stretching our body. As you open
and release tight, tense places in your body, know that your mind is
softening as well. We won't worry too much about which thoughts
are too tight and how they need to change just yet. We will simply
move and breathe and be aware of what comes to mind.

Daily Exercise: Stretching

Wear comfortable clothing and find an open space where you
have some room to move. You may want to lay a towel or mat
on the floor. Begin standing and simply stretch your hands up
over your head. If it feels good to bend back a little, enjoy that as
well. Notice which tight places find relief in this posture. Next,
reach down toward your toes for a forward fold. You don't have
to get all the way down or even lower your head past your heart
(especially if you have high blood pressure, glaucoma, or a cold).
What places feel tight as you move? Bring your hands to the floor
and lower down to a hands-and-knees position. Arch your back
up into a movement that resembles a hissing cat. Breathe deeply
and notice what gets stretched and how you respond. Come to
a seated position, and bring the soles of your feet together into
a cobbler's pose. You may fold forward (not down) if you wish.
Breathe deeply in this new position. Finally, lie on your back and
hug your knees in like a ball. You may rock a little from side to
side if this feels nice. Again, notice how your body feels as you
do this new position. You may lie flat on your back for a moment
to soak in the experience of stretching. Notice if your body feels

freer and more open. How about your mind? Gently come back up to a sitting position and then stand. You can return to these stretches anytime you wish.

Reflection

Our minds are landscapes with peaks and valleys. Many of them we know very well. Others may be over the horizon, requiring that we stretch a bit to see them. What do you notice in the landscape of your mind today?

The story of Peter and the food reminds us that we are not always able to see what is coming. Today begin jotting down a thought or two that you have about your anxiety. You are only asked to acknowledge the thought, not argue with it or prove it wrong. Many times in stretching, the first step is to feel where you are tight or tense. It is the same with our thoughts. Feel where the tightness and the strain exist. Write down a few thoughts about anxiety that you noticed in the last few minutes—not judging them, just noticing them.

_____

_____

_____

_____

_____

_____

_____

_____

_____

_____

_____

_____

_____

_____

_____

MOVEMENT WITHIN

Read Acts 9:1–22

> All who heard him were amazed and said, "Is not this
> the man who made havoc in Jerusalem among those who
> invoked [Jesus's] name? And has he not come here for the
> purpose of bringing them bound before the chief priests?"
> Saul became increasingly more powerful and confounded
> the Jews who lived in Damascus by proving that Jesus
> was the Messiah. (vv. 21–22)

THE STORY OF SAUL IS one of the more dramatic transformation
stories in the New Testament. The Spirit of Jesus Christ came
upon Saul in such a powerful way that just days after Saul had
encountered Jesus, people barely recognized him. It was as if he
was a new man. No longer was he persecuting Jesus's followers,
but instead he was proclaiming Jesus as Lord. No longer was he
puffed up with his own accomplishments, but now he was so
humble that he went more often by his Roman name Paul, which
has an underlying meaning of "small" or "humble," rather than
a name that recalled the first king of Israel. No longer was he
focused on keeping Judaism "pure" by rooting out followers of
Jesus, but instead he traveled to the ends of his known world to
bring more Gentiles into the early church.

As we heal from anxiety, we will find that the Spirit also trans-
forms us into new people. This transformation may not be instant
or as dramatic as what happened to Saul, but there will be a recog-
nizable change. There are core parts of us, our essence, and those
parts will remain, but there will be other habits and traits that
will change over time. We may move from being people who put

everyone else's needs ahead of our own—to the detriment of our health—to being people who make loving and caring for our own selves through exercise and relaxation a priority. We may change from being so overwhelmed that we are paralyzed to being active and on the move. We may transform from being people ruled by fear to being those with a spirit of courage and boldness.

These changes may seem distant and difficult now, but remember, with God's Spirit moving in our lives, nothing is impossible. Look around at the changes you have seen in others. Look at the changes that happen in the world around you—the very movement of life everywhere shows us that change is constant. For now, simply be open to the internal movement of God's Spirit. Acknowledge that it can be scary to think of yourself in a new way. But learn to trust that God's hand is moving in your life to bring about new life and purpose for you.

Daily Exercise: Move Around Outdoors

Use some form of movement outside in a place that is familiar to you. This could be as simple as taking a walk around your neighborhood or as interesting as going on a bike ride down a favorite trail. If your body is ready, you could even go for a run. Just get moving somewhere outside where you can observe your surroundings. As you move, take note of the things around you. What are the changes? Are there houses that have changed owners? Have new decorations been put up with the change of seasons? Are there new flowers blooming or are the leaves falling? As you notice the movement and change in the world outside you, consider what movement and change may be happening inside you. It probably will not be as dramatic as what happened to Saul on the Damascus road, but you also are being transformed.

Reflection

Change can be big or small. Today you were asked to change something about your movement and to observe change in your surroundings. Most of us will not experience the kind of dramatic change that Paul did, but we can notice what may need some change and then start planning for it.

As we move through the next few weeks, we will take more notice of our bodies, but we will also pay special attention to our thoughts. We will plan for change, not only in what we do physically and how we feel but in how we think as well.

Starting today, go back to some of the thoughts you had yesterday during your time of reflection or identify a nagging worry or anxious thought that sticks with you. Try to find one piece of evidence against that thought—that is, think of a time when the thing you worried about did not happen. We often worry, day after day after day, that some dreadful thing will happen, but day after day after day, it does not. So, even if what you notice is that the "bad thing" did not happen today, write it down.

DAY 6

MOVEMENT OF THE SPIRIT

Read Exodus 15:20-21

*Then the prophet Miriam, Aaron's sister, took a tambou-
rine in her hand; and all the women went out after her
with tambourines and with dancing. (v. 20)*

As we read in Exodus earlier this week, God delivered the Israelites from their bondage in Egypt through the waters of the Red
Sea. Shortly after their deliverance from oppression, Moses and
the Israelites sang a song of praise about God's coming to save
them and breathing freedom into their lives. As they sang, Miriam
and the other women played tambourines and danced in praise of
God's great redeeming work.

Transformative moments in our lives elicit movement in response. Think of how the exchange of wedding vows is often followed by dancing. The birth of a child usually brings hugs and
kisses all around. Even sorrow and grief have their own movements of bowing, grasping hands, or reaching out for what is no
longer there.

I did not grow up in a church that used much movement in
response to God's presence with us in weekly gatherings. We
mostly just sat quietly in our pews. Imagine my surprise when I
went to college and ended up in a somewhat charismatic student
fellowship, complete with tambourines, raised hands, and dancing! This new-to-me movement was actually quite refreshing. It
seemed that my body did want to do more than sit quietly in a
pew in response to God's activity in my life. Although I no longer
attend a charismatic church, I do still enjoy movement in response
to the Spirit's work in and around me. I traded my tambourine for

the bowing, kneeling, and genuflecting that accompany my current worship experience. I also feel the movement of prayer and praise when I practice yoga. The half sun salute alone is a wonderful body flow of adulation, prostration, engagement, and opening.

Are there ways you move in response to the Spirit's work? Are there profound, holy moments in your life that have led you to respond with movement? If not, consider what would feel like an authentic expression of movement to you. We might not all want to grab a tambourine and dance with Miriam, but we might find expression through kneeling or lowering ourselves in humility or opening ourselves up willingly to the presence of the Almighty One.

Daily Exercise: Yoga Flow

Wear comfortable clothing suitable for movement, and begin in a standing position. On an inhalation, lift your hands above your head. On an exhalation, tilt your upper body back in a slight backbend. Pause as you offer your open heart and hands to God in praise. On your next inhalation, come out of the backbend and then fold forward from the hips as you exhale. If you have a contraindication,[10] do not lower your head past your heart. Otherwise, bow yourself down, lowering your head and hands toward the ground. If you are uncomfortably tight, bend your knees a bit so you can concentrate on this movement of humility and submission to God. On your next inhalation, place your hands onto the floor outside of your feet (or on a chair seat in front of you for an easier movement). Move your right foot back on the mat. On your next exhalation, take the left foot back beside the right one and come down onto your knees. Then push your hips back toward your heels, lower your head to the ground, and extend your arms along your torso. This is called the child's pose. Think of how restful a sleeping baby is in this position, and while you remain in this position, release yourself to God's loving care. Then stretch forward onto your belly and lie prostrate for a moment. This is a classic pose for confession. Remain in this pose as you confess, then put your hands about a foot in front of you, keeping your forearms on the ground. Lift your head and heart forward to the sky in a gentle backbend (sphinx pose). In this pose, celebrate the new life that rises up in you. Then reverse the movements, taking yourself back to the folded child's pose. Then putting weight onto your hands, lift your tailbone in the air for a pose called the "downward-facing dog" or "down dog." From down dog, walk your feet forward for another standing forward fold. Then rise up with a strong core movement to finish with a final backbend, offering up your praise. Close with your hands folded in front of your heart, and pay attention to how your body and spirit feel after this moving prayer.

Reflection

Nearly every religious tradition uses some sort of movement in its worship. It may be as simple as sitting down and standing up or moving through the rituals surrounding the Lord's Supper. We move individually or we move together. God also moves in us, with us, and through us. As we finish this week of movement, consider what God's movement has been in you this week. Write down just one way that you have felt God moving in you, alongside you, or through you this week.

_____

_____

_____

_____

_____

_____

_____

_____

_____

_____

_____

_____

_____

_____

_____

_____

_____

_____

_____

_____

_____

_____

DAY 7

A COMMUNITY MOVES

Read Joshua 6

On the seventh day they rose early, at dawn, and marched around the city in the same manner seven times. It was only on that day that they marched around the city seven times. (v. 15)

THERE IS A LOT OF movement in Joshua 6 as the mass of Israelites marches around the city of Jericho in obedience to God's directions. For six days the people circled the city once, until the seventh day when they marched around it seven times.

All this marching around reminds me (Jason) of a Pascha service I attended while working in Richmond, Virginia. While in Richmond, I got to know an Eastern Orthodox priest named Father Andrew. We worked at the same homeless shelter site, each of us working two or three nights apiece. Occasionally we would talk, sometimes just to compare notes on the folks who were assigned to our shelter site.

Father Andrew was Eastern Orthodox, and I was Baptist. For me, Easter morning meant sitting outside on cold metal folding chairs at a sunrise service and singing "Christ the Lord Is Risen Today." For Father Andrew, it was different. I know because he invited me to Pascha one year at his church. Conveniently, most years the Orthodox calendar is a week or two later, so I did not even have to miss the cold folding chairs!

When I arrived at four o'clock in the morning, there were people who had been sleeping in the church since the night before. The place was dark, with just enough candles lit to help you find your way to the main room with its icon of Christ—a large painting with Jesus, halo around his head, as he made a sign of blessing with his fingers. The people who had spent the night were beginning to awaken. No one spoke out loud. There was only whispering. I eventually connected with Father Andrew and greeted him with a whisper. I remember how disorienting, but somewhat exciting, the whole moment was. Everyone sat or lay on the floor—waking, watching, waiting for something to happen.

Then there was what seemed like a sudden conspiracy of whispers. People got up, and we made our way outside. Each of us was given a candle in the dark. We lit them, one by one, and then walked around the house that was their church—all of us, walking around and around and around the building. Seven times we walked around it, just as the children of Israel did in Joshua.

Then Father Andrew knocked on the door, opening it, and all of us with our candles filed into the sanctuary, filling the dim space with light. Spontaneously people, no longer whispering, called to each other in clear, strong tones, "Christ is risen!" Others responded, "He is risen indeed!" Over and over and over again we said it. "Christ is risen!" "He is risen indeed!"

When I think about the community of faith moving as one, speaking as one, singing as one, I think of that Pascha celebration. I also think of Joshua instructing the Israelites to march around the city, over and over again, day after day. As God's people gather, his mysterious presence shows up to tear down walls and raise the dead. And while I have certainly experienced God individually, far from the doors of a church, I still need the community of faith. We all need the community of faith. We need to move together as a community, carrying light into places of darkness, proclaiming the truth of our faith, proclaiming the sort of life that emerges out of death. The first reaction of people at the grave was fear (or, we might say, anxiety), and the angel at the tomb told them, "Do not be afraid"—just as God said to Joshua, "Do not be afraid!" Take heart in the strength and courage that your community brings!

Daily Exercise: Move with Others

This chapter has focused on movement, but for the most part, it has been movement done alone. Today see if you can find a person or a group of people with whom to move. Perhaps this is a day of worship for you. If so, call some friends and see if they would like to go on a walk before or after church. If this is not a day you would normally get together with others, go ahead and connect with friends to walk or run or ride together. Depending on the size of your community, you may even be able to find a running group or cycling group to join. These can be great ways to enjoy community, but they are also excellent ways to get support as you try to make changes in your life.

Reflection

Jason remembers his Eastern Orthodox celebration of Pascha as a time when the community moved in unison to strengthen one another and build courage. Think back to a time when being part of a community emboldened you to face some darkness or brought you glimpses of light. How might your community do that for you now in your present circumstances?

_____

_____

_____

_____

_____

_____

_____

_____

_____

_____

_____

_____

CHAPTER 3 REVIEW

Was there a day or movement exercise that particularly appealed to you?

Was there a particular type of movement that was challenging to you?

Was there a moment this week where you were proud of yourself or surprised yourself in a good way?

Was there any part of you that experienced a shifting this week? A move from inertia to forward motion?

Was there any part of you that resisted this forward motion? Why did it resist?

Without judgment or criticism, think of how you are able to approach movement in your life right now. If you have not moved in a while and this task is challenging, that is okay. Just acknowledge that truth. If you have debilitating conditions like arthritis or chronic pain, acknowledge that. Whatever your current situation is, be okay with it. Approach this upcoming session with hope for finding the right level and amount of movement for you at this time. There is no winning or failing in these attempts. There is just moving one step forward from where you are—again and again. Try to think of where that next move forward will be.

CHAPTER 4

MIND

DAY 1

MANAGING THE MIND

Read 2 Timothy 1:1–14

*For God has not given us a spirit of fear, but of power
and of love and of a sound mind. (v. 7 NKJV)*

AS MUCH AS IT FEELS like I battle my body in the height of my
anxiety, my mind can be an even greater challenge in the fight
against fear. Even people without anxiety disorders often wrestle with the continuing distractions and runaway worries of their
minds. Add to this the scary and damaging thoughts that play
through the mind of an anxiety sufferer and you have a setup for
struggle.

However, it does not have to be this way. As Paul reminds us,
God does not want us to live in fear or be held back in shame over
our struggles. Instead, we are encouraged to reach out to God in
search of sound teaching and truths to which we can anchor our
thoughts. Our minds were not created to be minefields of anxiety
but rather to be sound vehicles through which we can experience
God's power and love.

How do we move from the battle zone of fear to a sound mind?
Today, we will begin this journey of seeking calm in the storms
of our minds by simply linking breath with prayer. I have found
the breath prayer in today's exercise to be a favorite tool when
I feel my anxiety levels rise. If I am approaching a situation or
a time that is triggering my anxiety, I shift into breath prayer.
I can feel my breath steady as I breathe and recite "Lord Jesus
Christ, have mercy on me" again and again. If things are particularly tense, I may even revert to my shortened, more Southern
version of the prayer, "Lawd, have mercy." Either way this saving

thought slowly crowds the worries out of my mind. Although it does not send the anxiety completely away, it lessens it enough to be manageable.

Daily Exercise: Breath Prayer

The breath prayer is the linking of a simple sentence with the inhalation and exhalation of breath. One of the most classic breath prayers is the Jesus Prayer: pray "Lord Jesus Christ" on inhalation and "have mercy on me" on exhalation. This sentence is prayed over and over in rhythm with your breath. Before you start the breath prayer, pick a sentence that has meaning for you. It can be as simple as "God, help me" or as nuanced and specific as you wish. Pick a name of God and an action for which you seek his help. For instance, I could pick the name "Jesus" and the action I seek as "bring peace." My prayer would then be [inhale] "Jesus," [exhale] "bring peace."

When you are ready to practice the breath prayer, find a comfortable position where you will have quiet for a few minutes. Come to an awareness of your breath and fall into a gentle belly breath. Now add the phrase to your breath. Breathe this simple prayer repeatedly for the next few minutes. When you are finished with your breath prayer practice, return to normal breathing and notice any differences in your body and mind from when you began. The beauty of the breath prayer is that you can take it with you throughout your day, coming back to it again and again when you need its calming focus for your rattled mind.

Reflection

As we work toward better management of anxious thoughts, we have started again with the breath. While this may seem peculiar, learning to soothe the body helps us better manage soothing the mind. This works in multiple ways. Diaphragmatic breathing (e.g., belly breathing) triggers the parasympathetic nervous system and soothes an overstimulated body. Focusing on a word or phrase as you follow the breath allows you to return to that word or phrase when your thoughts move toward anxious patterns of thinking, such as *What if _____ happens?* Rather than following your anxious thoughts, return to the breath. I have often encouraged people to think of their thoughts as "just thoughts"—they are not all of who you are. And many times, they are just passing by.

In addition, focusing on your body, breath, and specific physical sensations actually changes the pathway of your thinking. Our brains tend to overgeneralize when we feel stress or anxiety, turning a thought such as *This is difficult* into *This will always be difficult.* Focusing on your breath and body instead of your mind helps you come back to the present moment, seeing a particular situation as difficult instead of *every* situations as *always* difficult.

In today's reflection, I urge you to think of your breath prayer phrase as a pathway toward something calm or positive or peaceful. Avoid negative phrases, such as "God, take away this fear." Removing the fear is certainly our desire, but saying it in this way reminds us of the worry rather than allowing us to move toward peace. Consider your breath prayer phrase a light that leads you forward, away from the danger that may (or may not) lurk behind you.

In the space below, prayerfully write down the phrase or phrases you used in the exercise or phrases you might use in the future.

_____

_____

_____

_____

_____

_____

_____

_____

_____

DAY 2

IMPACT OF THE MIND

Read Psalm 77

In the day of my trouble I seek the Lord; in the night my hand is stretched out without wearying; my soul refuses to be comforted. (v. 2)

THIS LAMENT PSALM ILLUSTRATES THAT the struggle with anxious thoughts is nothing new. The psalmist has worried all day and night, and all he can do now is moan. No amount of thinking or praying has brought comfort. Instead of finding an answer, he has only more questions and worry. *Is God angry? Has God forgotten me? Will I be miserable forever?*

The mind is a wonderful gift, but when worry takes root, its power can be destructive. *Hmm, I have a tingling sensation in my chest. I wonder what that is.* We think and worry about the tingling, and the brain, sensing danger, produces more adrenaline and cortisol. The stress hormones take their effect, and the tingling increases. *Oh no,* we think, *it's worse. What if something is really wrong?*

We wonder what caused this strange feeling. A pulled muscle? What if it's cancer . . . or a heart attack? We massage the tingling area as we review heart attack symptoms and remember when we last had our cholesterol checked. The more we focus on the possible problem, the worse we feel. As our mind misreads our body's signals, it gets harder to sort out what is really happening. The runaway train of anxiety starts and getting off it often requires outside help.

An important management technique is breaking the cycle of escalation. We see it happening in Psalm 77. After cycling through anxious thoughts to the point of misery, the psalmist changes his tone. Instead of replaying his present worries, the psalmist reaches back and recalls God's good works. He calls to mind very specific acts where God brought order and safety. He goes back to the waters of chaos at creation, noting that these threatening waters were afraid of God. The psalmist remembers that God brings order to unruly threats and makes paths through the sea. What once brought fear can bring new life instead.

Shifting your thought process like this is one way to break a cycle of fear. Another way is practice deep breathing or do a full body scan to reconnect with more than just your worrisome parts. You might go outside or watch a favorite movie to distract yourself with positive stimuli. Many practices can help break the cycle so we can bring ourselves back to a calmer state.

Daily Exercise: Progressive Muscle Relaxation in Body and Mind

While anxious thinking has a negative effect on the body, focusing your mind on your body can also have a positive effect. Today you will use progressive muscle relaxation to allow your mind to soothe and calm your body. Find a comfortable position lying on your back where you can be uninterrupted for fifteen minutes. Start by taking a few cleansing breaths.

Begin with the feet and work your way upward. Flex your feet and then tighten your calves, thighs, and all your leg muscles. Lift your legs an inch off the ground and tighten them as much as you can. Let it all go, letting your legs drop down to the ground. Think about how the muscle release felt.

Next, tighten your hands into fists. Tighten your biceps, triceps, and all the muscles in your hands and arms. Lift your arms an inch off the ground and tighten them as much as you can. Let it all go, releasing your arms and hands down to the ground. Squeeze your butt muscles and then let them relax. Hunch your shoulders up to your ears and then relax them down and back to the floor. Take a deep belly breath, and release the air with a cleansing sigh. Lengthen your face by raising your eyebrows, opening your mouth, and sticking out your tongue. Make a prune face, and then relax the muscles. Feel the release of the muscles in your face and the rest of the muscle groups you have tightened and released.

Now, you will repeat the exercise mentally. Think of your feet, as if you are observing them. Mentally remind them to relax. Think of your legs, noticing them as if there were a spotlight on them. Remind them to sink into the ground. In the same way, remind your hands and arms, your back and shoulders. If you are lying down, mentally remind the whole weight of your head to rest on the floor. Let your neck be soft—jaw dropping open slightly, tongue resting in your palate, eyes sinking back into their sockets. Review your whole body, noticing any remaining tension. Send a breath there and let it release. Just as the ground holds your entire body easily and gladly, so does God. Rest for a few minutes, mindful of being held. When you are ready to awaken from your rest, deepen your breath gradually, wiggle your fingers and toes, and turn on your side for a moment before slowly rising. Take a moment to notice how your body and mind feel after this relaxation exercise.

Reflection

This section has at least two important elements. The first is the pattern of many lament psalms. The crying out is fully voiced, and then the psalmist turns—remembering God's help in the past and expecting that he will help again. Lament psalms remind us that God wants to hear us voice our worries and concerns. Today we focused on the turn, recalling specific ways God has been with us before. This helps us see our present difficulty as a problem we have now, not as something that will *always* be a problem.

The second point is a reminder to focus on your physical self. This practice is another way of moving toward the specific from the general, and then allowing our thoughts to follow.

Try to write down two things. Write down a past event where you have seen God's provision and protection. Be as specific as you can. Then write down what physical/bodily sensation helps ground you. Write two or three if you can. Think of things that help you be in the present, not in the swirl of thoughts, such as twirling a pen, receiving or giving a hug, or petting the dog.

MOVEMENT OF THE MIND

Read Matthew 14:22–33

By this time the boat, battered by the waves, was far from the land, for the wind was against them. (v. 24)

IF YOU PAY MUCH ATTENTION to your mind, you will notice it rarely is quiet. This is not just true for those who deal with anxiety but for everyone. Thoughts flow through our minds like waves.

Anxiety comes into play when a thought that causes us worry or fear rolls through our mind. When we are prone to anxiety, the thought becomes sticky. We have trouble not getting caught up in it. Then because we are having such trouble letting the thought roll by, we become anxious that we will never be rid of the thought. When anxiety is attached to the thought, it seems to become stronger, more intense, and more difficult to allow to pass from our mind, as most other thoughts are apt to do.

In this way we are like Peter in our reading today. At the beginning of the reading Peter is in the boat, floating amid the waves. As the waves roll through the sea, they rock the boat. When the waves get bigger and scarier, they toss the boat to and fro. Then Jesus comes and invites Peter to walk *on* the waves, preventing him from being tossed about by their power. Peter starts out, but then a thought frightens him. The wind. When Peter focused on the wind, his fear gained power and he began to sink in the waves.

We also get tossed back and forth by our thoughts sometimes. But there is another way. God invites us to rise above our thoughts and walk on top of the waves that roll through our mind. As long as no particular thought grabs our attention, especially a fearful thought, we are fine. But even when a fearful thought attaches itself to us and we begin to sink into the deep, God comes and lifts us up again.

Another way of thinking about this is the image we used earlier of consciousness as if it were a churning sea. Different thoughts surface from the deep waters and then dip below the surface. Just because a particular thought surfaces does not mean it represents all of who we are. It is one thought among many—it just happens to be one that broke the surface of the murky water, for a brief time.

Some describe this as the mind offering us different thoughts to grab and play with. Thousands of thoughts go through our minds during the course of a day, but over time, the mind realizes we prefer certain thoughts more than others. When a thought is offered, we grab it and roll it around for a while. If we choose a thought repeatedly, it can become a pattern that our mind likes to follow. During a pause in thinking my mind may remember, "Oh, she likes to worry about her children. She grabs this thought quickly and wrings it round and round like her hands. I'll see if she wants to hold this thought now." But in the end, my worry over my children is just one thought among many. If I could learn not to grab it, this specific worry would pass along with all the other thoughts that roll through my mind in a day.

The first step is learning not to let these "thought storms" control us. Remember that as humans we have many thoughts that come *and* go. As we practice observing the thoughts, we will try to watch them instead of grabbing and holding them. This will lessen the power of these thoughts over our lives.

Daily Exercise: Mindfulness Meditation

Find a comfortable sitting or lying-down position. You may want to set a timer for ten minutes so you can relax and not worry about time. Attend to your breath and notice your body settle into whatever position you have chosen. Focus on your breathing while letting your thoughts go. A thought will arise very soon. As it does, acknowledge it and then let it float away like a cloud in the wind.

Keep breathing and observing your thoughts as they pass by, without any particular thought grabbing you. If you notice that a certain "sticky" thought comes up and grabs your attention, gently let the thought go. Bring your attention back to the rhythm and flow of your breathing. Keep repeating this process anytime you notice you have traveled down a particular thought's trail. Don't beat yourself up or be frustrated that a thought has grabbed you. This is normal and happens to everyone. Just keep returning to your breathing and the process of observing the chatter of your mind without having to engage in any particular thought or idea. You may or may not feel relaxed, and you may even worry whether this meditation is working. Successful meditation does not mean you immediately feel peaceful or that you do not struggle with your thoughts. It simply means you have made the time and commitment to practice the awareness of your mental chatter and the release of your thoughts. If at any time you get overly upset or frustrated, release yourself from the practice without fear of failure. If you are still in meditation when your alarm goes off, let your breath deepen a bit and gently bring yourself back to the awareness of your surroundings.

Reflection

What are your "sticky" thoughts? What types of thoughts are the ones you seem to turn over and over when they arise? Write them down here so you can recognize them. The trick is to treat such thoughts as if they were people at a party you do not want to speak to. It helps to at least nod in their direction but then move away so you do not get caught in that difficult conversation. Jot down the "names" of those who usually show up at the "worry party."

_____

_____

_____

_____

_____

_____

CHAPTER 4: MIND

DAY 4
AWARENESS OF THE MIND

Read Luke 15:11–24

But when he came to himself he said, "How many of my father's hired hands have bread enough and to spare, but here I am dying of hunger!" (v. 17)

OUR MINDS CAN TAKE US to some pretty rough places. In this passage from Luke, the younger son's thoughts have led him to ask for his inheritance and travel far away from home (*Anywhere else has got to be better than here*). Then when things didn't work out in the foreign land and the son was starving, his thoughts led to him taking a job feeding pigs (*I have no choice; I am a failure*). But there in the mud and muck with the pigs, the proverbial bottom which the son hit, something interesting happened. The son began to wake up. He realized there was another choice. He could go home again. Though the son believed his failures and brokenness made him unworthy to be his father's son, he could at least work as a servant in his father's house.

Like this younger son, our thoughts can take us to difficult and even destructive places. I used to have a habit of talking very negatively to myself about myself. When I made a mistake, I'd tell myself, "You are so stupid, you can't do anything right." On hard days I'd say, "Things will never get better; it will always be this hard." Such self-critical thoughts led me down the road to anxiety and depression. It was not until I was raising our small children and making great effort to speak to them with kindness and love that I woke up one day and became aware of how negatively I was talking to myself.

When the contrast between my outward language to my children and my inner language to myself became clear, I realized how much I had unwittingly damaged my mind and spirit. Then I made the connection between how I talked to myself and how I felt.

We can find ourselves sunk in the negative and destructive chatter in our minds, just as the prodigal son found himself penned in with the pigs. During my moments of negative and critical self-talk, the redemption of my mind was challenging because I saw myself as anything but a child of God—at least in what I was saying to myself about myself.

Removing ourselves from this muck is hard. The first step, and a challenging one, is to really look at the mud that covers us—that is, negative thought patterns. There are several common negative thought patterns in people who struggle with anxiety:

- Viewing events in the past, present, or future with all-or-nothing language
- Believing we either have to be perfect or we are a "total mess"
- Allowing no in-between when it comes to our evaluation of ourselves or others
- Engaging in catastrophic thinking, where a small headache is a brain tumor, a tingling in our chest is an impending heart attack, and so on
- Using words like *never* and *always* to describe ourselves and so evaluate ourselves in stable, never-changing ways

You may not have trouble with all of these negative thoughts, but you probably encounter some of them. The first step in freeing ourselves from our own negative core thoughts is to identify what they are and become aware of how they influence us.

And, dear ones, unlike the prodigal son, you may not have grown up in a loving home or been surrounded by kind people. Negative messages in your head may have been given to you by someone else—a critical parent, a spouse, or a bully during childhood.

These unhelpful messages are not your fault. Your task now is to take note of them and name them as hurtful. Once you identify the thoughts as hurtful, you can begin to wash them away, working to heal your mind and replace these old mucky messages with the grace and love of a God who waits for you at the end of the road.

Daily Exercise: Take Notice of Your Core Thoughts

Our core thoughts take on regular forms for us. They may be directed inward and be about your safety, whether you are truly worthy of love, or whether you can be effective and competent in the world. Sometimes the thoughts are directed outward, as you think about others and what might happen to them.

Today listen with intention for your core thoughts. Notice what you say when (not if) you make a mistake. Do you say, "I'm such an idiot"? Or, "Oh no! They are going to get killed doing that"? Are those worried thoughts about someone seeing you in a way that would be embarrassing or isolating? Are those statements you say under your breath about loved ones?

Whatever these thoughts are, your job today is to write them down, to identify the mud you may be stuck in. Take a notecard wherever you go today, and jot down a word or two that reminds you of what you said to yourself throughout the day. Pull the card out occasionally to remind you of this task for the day.

Reflection

We all have comments we make, often under our breath. The notecard approach (or using an electronic version) helps because you have taken something that is a habit and asked your brain to pay a different sort of attention to it. The area of our brain that handles habits is the basal ganglia, but the area of our brain that pays attention to our life is different. It is the prefrontal cortex. It is a good thing that habits get stored in another location so you do not have to decide every day which shoe to put on first or how you will brush your teeth this time. Habits help us . . . except when they are the negative thoughts that keep us mired in worry and anxiety.

When you jot down your thoughts, you are changing where these thoughts are located in the brain. This way the thoughts move to an area where you can reconsider them and not just follow the habit or script.

Consider carrying this exercise forward a few days or even a week, just to make sure those habitual thoughts become more open to change. Our first step is to take note of the muck that we are in; our next step will be to see what we can do to get out! Use this space to write down core thoughts you notice through your day, especially the ones that are more emotionally laden.

_____

_____

_____

_____

_____

_____

_____

_____

_____

_____

_____

_____

_____

_____

_____

_____

_____

_____

_____

_____

_____

_____

_____

DAY 5

REDEEMING THE MIND

Read Luke 15:11–32
"This son of mine was dead and is alive again; he was lost and is found!" And they began to celebrate. (v. 24)

JUST BECAUSE WE HAVE A thought does not mean it is necessarily true. Today's reading continues from reading yesterday's when the prodigal thought he was no longer worthy to be called his father's son. But as the parable demonstrates, the son's thought was not true. The loving father ran to greet his son before the boy ever reached home. No mistake could ever erase the father's love for his son, no matter what the prodigal had believed.

I wonder how long it took for the prodigal to start thinking a new thought—the thought that he belonged in his father's home as a beloved son. Was it when his dad kissed him? When he put new shoes on the son's dirty feet? When the father ate with the son at the table during the feast held in his honor? I also wonder how the son's changed thinking affected his relationship with his father. Once he knew he was unconditionally loved and forgiven, did his love for his father deepen? Was he finally able to enjoy the abundance of life in his father's house? Were there other ways in which he was brought back to life?

It takes time to rewrite a damaging thought and even more time to heal from its effects. This is especially true when the thought is one we have told ourselves over and over. The first step, as we already discussed, is identifying our most common negative thoughts. Next, we need to test our thoughts to see if they are helpful or accurate. If a thought falls in the category of core negative thoughts, then the thought probably needs to be released and *replaced* with a new, healing thought that reflects the love of the Father we see in the parable.

The good news is that thoughts are often just habits. We get accustomed to thinking a certain way, of believing certain messages to be true. When we realize a habit is destructive to our well-being, we must take steps to change it. God's Word can be a powerful antidote to the untruths of our core negative thoughts. We can hold redeeming messages deep within us and call them to mind when destructive thoughts intrude. Today we will dig into God's Word and allow it to speak healing words of goodness and truth into our brokenness. Over time this practice of calling Scripture to mind will become second nature, replacing negative speech with words of God's grace and love.

Daily Exercise: Scripture Memorization

Today we will spend some time sifting through Scripture and preparing for the discipline of Scripture memorization. First, review your core negative thoughts. As we have learned, there is a good chance these messages do not speak goodness or truth into your life and are preventing you from living in the fullness of God's love and grace. If you are well acquainted with Scripture, allow a particular passage to come to mind that expresses a greater truth than your negative thought. For example, if you have the negative thought *My life will always be bad*, then look to Jeremiah 29: "I know the plans I have for you . . . plans to prosper you and not to harm you, plans to give you hope and a future" (v. 11 NIV) If you are not very familiar with Scripture, you can take some sample verses from the following list. Even better, start exploring God's Word to see what it has to say to you.

Once you have found a word that speaks goodness and truth to you, commit it to memory. Write it on a sticky note and put it on the mirror. Write it on an index card and keep it on the dashboard of your car. You can even take Deuteronomy 11 literally and write the words on your hand! Put God's Word where you can read it again and again until it is written on your heart and soul. Once this happens, God's sword (Eph. 6:17) will cut the negative thoughts that bind you and set you free. Here are some examples:

Common Negative Core Thoughts	Corresponding Scripture
I will always be alone.	Psalm 23:4
I am ugly and worthless.	Genesis 1:27
It will never be the same.	Isaiah 43:19
They will never accept me.	Psalm 27:10
I am broken.	Isaiah 43:1
I always mess up.	John 3:17
I am being punished.	Romans 8:28
God is far from me.	Revelation 21:3–4
This is going to be much worse than I think.	Isaiah 40:31
It will never get better.	Isaiah 43:19
I am never going to get this right.	Philippians 4:13
I am so weak.	2 Corinthians 12:9
I will always be disappointed.	Jeremiah 29:11

Reflection

The father in the story was waiting at the end of the road, not with anger or condemnation but with arms of love. Even then, it probably took time and gentle reminders for the son to believe that his acceptance was true.

Our typical anxious instinct is to fight or flee when we encounter something negative. But when we try to fight a negative thought, we inadvertently give it *more* power—much like the old adage says, "Never wrestle with a pig. You get dirty and besides, the pig likes it." By giving a negative thought more attention than it deserves, we reinforce the path that leads to it.

What gesture could you make internally or externally that would be gentle and releasing to a negative thought instead of combative? Maybe it is deep breathing in with the Scripture you are memorizing and then breathing out to release the negative thought. Maybe it is a hand gesture of gently pushing away the negative and pulling God's words of grace and love toward you. Consider how you might allow the thought to be washed away instead of being something you fight against.

DAY 6

RETRAINING THE MIND

Read Philippians 4:4–14

Finally, beloved, whatever is true, whatever is honorable, whatever is just, whatever is pure, whatever is pleasing, whatever is commendable, if there is any excellence and if there is anything worthy of praise, think about these things. (v. 8)

CERTAIN THOUGHTS AND PATTERNS OF thinking become habits. In Dena's yoga training, she learned about how repetitive thoughts and actions make little grooves in our mind like grooves in a field. Jason's reading in the psychological and neuroscience literature has found similar information. When stress arises, our thinking is likely to follow well-worn grooves, like rainwater finding a well-worn path in a field. This is why we revert back to the same worries or negative habits when we feel tense.

Because of this, it is important in anxiety management not just to diminish the power of negative thinking but to build the habit of positive thinking. We need to make new grooves in our brain for our thoughts to travel down naturally. This will take some time but will be well worth the effort.

Today we will take Paul's advice in Philippians 4 and begin the habit of focusing on what is true and excellent and praiseworthy instead of ruminating on what is hurtful and harmful. Even Paul acknowledges that we have to keep practicing our focus on Christlike things for change to come. Over time practicing this habit will transform not only our thinking but our very souls.

Returning to the language about the way our thoughts can form a "path," it can be helpful to think of our walk with God as a journey. There was certainly a beginning point to that journey, whether it was when you were a child or an adult. But following that path and acknowledging it can be winding and difficult at times is important too. The longer we keep walking with God, which includes the content of our thoughts, the easier those steps become.

Daily Exercise: Gratitude Journal

Ann Voskamp, author of *One Thousand Gifts*, encourages us to write down everything that is good and praiseworthy during the course of each day. When she began to practice this habit, her goal was to record such events until she reached one thousand "gifts." She wrote down both the small blessings and the large.

Today write down everything for which you are grateful—the big things, like a promotion at work or going on vacation, as well as the smallest of gifts, such as drinking a good cup of coffee or seeing a pretty sunrise. Maybe your beloved takes you to dinner or a friend gives you a compliment. Take note of every good, true, pure, and pleasing thing that you can find. Start the day with a blank piece of paper or computer screen. Then look for all that is worthy of giving thanks, right in the midst of your everyday life.

Of course you will encounter some hard moments as well, but today you will look for as much good as you can, even in the midst of difficulty. You may be surprised at how quickly your list grows. At the end of the day, take note of the items that are a part of your daily life. Try to retain your eye for gratitude when you encounter these things in the days to come.

Reflection

Our God-given brains work in funny ways at times! But when you understand the "why" behind it, these confounding ways have a logic to them.

Psychological science offers an interesting lesson through an experiment in which people completed a maze by drawing a line from start to finish. They did so by taking on the role of a mouse pictured on the sheet of paper. But there were two versions of the maze. One version had an image of a mouse running from a hungry owl. The other maze had the image of the mouse moving toward a yummy piece of cheese.

The subjects finished drawing their way through the maze in about the same amount of time. That was not where the difference was. Following completion of the maze, the subjects completed a test that measured their creativity. As you might guess, those who completed the maze with the owl (which is a more fear-based task) scored lower on their creativity. Those who were moving toward the cheese (called an "approach" mentality) were much more creative.

This helps explain the "why" behind the gratitude exercise. Thanksgiving (gratitude) helps us move forward in expectation; fear (anxiety) leads us to shut off options, to think less creatively. In addition to doing the exercise, I want you to think of *when and where you may feel more creative.* Jot down what is happening at these times. Is there less stress? Is there more fun? Also think about when you feel trapped or closed in. What is it about these situations that may do you well to avoid, or how can you inject more gratitude or goodness in these places?

_____

_____

_____

_____

_____

_____

_____

_____

_____

_____

_____

SHARING OUR THOUGHTS

Read Galatians 6:1–5

*Bear one another's burdens, and in this way you will ful-
fill the law of Christ. (v. 2)*

BEING OPEN WITH OTHERS IS often a difficult step to take. If you
are reading this in the context of a small group, then you have
likely taken the first step. It means taking risks, but taking the risk
of being open with others is what we are called to do.

Many years ago I read a powerful sermon by Barbara Brown
Taylor in *The Christian Century*. She drew from the Luke 13 passage where Jesus says he would gather Jerusalem like a mother hen
gathers her defenseless baby chicks, protecting them from preda-
tors that would seek to hurt, kill, and eat them. Taylor explains
how the "mother hen" offered herself up so the chicks could
escape the fox who had come to plunder and kill. She describes
the hen, "wings spread, breast exposed" and notes "if you mean
what you say, then this is how you stand."[11] The image of Jesus,
arms open, nailed to a cross should be obvious.

It is a challenge of our faith that the way is one of openness and
vulnerability. Paul writes in 1 Corinthians that this confounds the
"wisdom" of the world. It makes me shake my head too.

The Galatian church had seen some division. Some people
followed the Jewish law of circumcision, and there were others
who did not. Paul worked hard to explain, "There is no Jew, nor
Greek," meaning that they were all one in Christ. And then later
he writes to them, "Bear one another's burdens."

There were disagreements in the early church, just as there are
disagreements now. Supporting someone on their journey with

God means listening for understanding. That sort of listening often means holding our own reactions and retorts, especially if we disagree. As others have noted, we can disagree without being disagreeable. "Bearing the burden" of a fellow Christ follower will not always mean agreeing, but it does mean being open and accepting of that person as a fellow child of God.

This way of openness is the way of support. Many people are afraid to share the hurtful things that have happened to them. It takes being vulnerable. But if we are never open about our worries and our fears, how will we ever know the comfort of a fellow traveler as they help us, hold us, and support us? And even though it can feel risky to share, this is a risk we are called to take.

Daily Exercise: Share Struggles with a Friend and Invite Feedback

We often keep our thoughts and worries locked securely inside, but this only allows them to fester and grow. If we can share them with a trusted friend, it can lessen their power over us. Chances are good that our friends will not react with judgment or apathy but with compassion.

Think of one or two people with whom you would feel safe sharing one of your worries or struggles. Be discerning about who you choose. Someone who has not been supportive of you in the past or is the source of your anxiety may not be the best choice. Instead choose a friend you view as compassionate, wise, and trustworthy. Pick one struggle or fear you feel comfortable sharing with them and then take the step to make contact. You may wish to talk by phone or set up a coffee date so you can speak face-to-face.

This act of sharing just one fear will go a long way toward breaking down the stigma and shame of anxiety for you. You will probably feel relief when you finally share your thoughts. If you get emotional when speaking with your friend, remember that tears are okay to share too. We are human beings, and our emotions are part of what makes us the beautiful, complicated creatures we were meant to be. If things go well and you feel comfortable, you might invite your friend to give you some feedback on your fear or struggle. They may offer a refreshing perspective you could not have arrived at on your own. Even if your sharing does not go exactly as you hoped, know that the very act of taking the step to share a burden is a success for you. Sharing your burdens may take some practice for both you and the people around you.

Reflection

Write a few lines about the experience of being vulnerable in the way you were asked to do in today's exercise. Remember, the power God showed us through Christ was not a power of this world. Instead this power was one that was humble and open. Ideally, Christian community is the place where we can be vulnerable with our hopes and fears (though, as many of us know, churches can often be places where vulnerability is punished). Write about the good parts of today's exercise or other times when being open and vulnerable resulted in something good.

_____

_____

_____

_____

_____

_____

_____

_____

_____

_____

_____

_____

_____

CHAPTER 4 REVIEW

What exercise this week was most helpful to you?

Which exercise was most challenging?

What were your sticky thoughts?

Were you able to identify a core negative thought?

Did you notice times when you were angry or frustrated with yourself about your negative thoughts? If so, what is something gentle you can say to yourself to remember that this is a practice and will take time?

Imagine yourself as a child who is trying to learn something new. What is a good way to encourage rather than scold?

Mindfulness meditation can feel a little awkward until you have practiced it a few times. List any questions or concerns about your meditation exercise. If you are reading this book with a group, ask these during class time. If not, share with a friend who is also practicing meditation.

CHAPTER 5

CHANGE

DAY 1

CHANGING BEGINS WITH THE BREATH

Read 2 Peter 1:19–22

No prophecy ever came by human will, but men and women moved by the Holy Spirit spoke from God. (v. 21)

THE PROPHETS OF THE OLD Testament were pretty unpopular people. As God's servants living out their calling as messengers of the God-breathed word for the people of their times, the prophets more often than not spoke words of change. And one thing that is true of people throughout the centuries is that we are resistant to change—even good, Spirit-led change.

Still the Spirit moves to help us past our resistance. We may be nervous and unsure about a new message, but God is the relentless pursuer of humankind, breathing words of salvation and life. Eventually some of us stiff-necked people relent and take in this new God breath. We inhale and allow his message of salvation to sweep through us, even when we know it will mean change.

The biggest changes in our life are often preceded by a deep breath. A deep inhalation and a long sigh release our resistance as we take those first steps of a new way. "Yes, I'll marry you." "Okay, we'll make that move." "Yes, I finally agree to seek some help."

You may have noticed yourself struggling with resistance as you have gone through these weeks of daily practices. You may have heard calls to change that you were not sure you wanted to answer. Then again, if you take a minute to look back, you might notice that change has already snuck up on you. There may already be habits shifting or thoughts softening and beginning to be remade.

Still, there is a sense of newness to this journey. The steps farther ahead may still be unclear. The lamp only lights the next step,
and the morning star has not yet risen, much less the sun. But if
you trust your breath and the One who sends it—two constants
no matter what your journey entails—you will hold steady.

So today we look back from whence we came, we look forward
to what lies ahead, and we let out a sigh of release to one of the
inevitable forces of life—change.

Daily Exercise: Breath of Release

For today's breathing exercise you will focus on exhalation. Only
when you have fully emptied yourself of what you have been holding in, and on to, will you be fully open and receptive to the new,
fresh breath that waits to fill you.

In a comfortable position, begin by focusing on your breath.
When you are ready, deepen your release of the breath. Then focus
on your next exhalation. Let it out with a sigh. On your next
inhalation, simply allow yourself to receive the *pneuma* (Greek
for "spirit," "wind," "breath") that waits to fill you. Continue
with this focus on full exhalation, also allowing yourself to open
up and receive each subsequent breath. With each exhalation, you
may want to consciously release some thought or some event or
some hurt you have been holding. Or you may want to let go of
some internal resistance. On your inhalations, try adopting a true
spirit of openness as you receive the breath of change. You could
include hand motions to symbolize these intentions: on exhalation extend your palms out facing downward with an attitude of
releasing and on inhalation turn them upward to receive.

Reflection

Sometimes change is happening but we just have not noticed it
yet. Where do you see a little bit of change? You may note something new that is happening. Were there times when you noticed
you did not react to a situation as you normally might have? Make

a note of the absence of worry or anxiety. Maybe the change you notice is affected by your breathing. Remember that the breathing exercises trigger your parasympathetic nervous system. Note the changes in your breath, your body, your thoughts, or your spirit.

_____

_____

_____

_____

_____

_____

_____

_____

_____

_____

_____

_____

_____

_____

_____

_____

_____

_____

_____

_____

_____

_____

_____

_____

_____

_____

CHANGING BODY HABITS

Read 1 Corinthians 6:19–20

Do you not know that your body is a temple of the Holy Spirit within you, which you have from God, and that you are not your own? (v. 19)

SEVERAL WEEKS AGO WE ASKED you to think about how you were treating your body. That may have been one of those moments of resistance for you as you considered what it would be like to cut out your second cup of morning coffee or your nightly sweet. But maybe you did make some changes over the past few weeks. Maybe some of them felt good, and maybe others were harder than you wanted them to be. Maybe the thought of one of the changes in diet, sleep, or exercise was so unpleasant you never even tried it.

Let's go back to one or two of the body changes you felt the most resistance toward. Was it your sleep habits? Your caffeine consumption? Giving up sweets? The exercise? Whatever the sticking point was, let us just dwell there for a moment. Think about this matter as a way God can manifest his grace toward you rather than laying down a law you have to follow. After all, your body was given to you as a gift from God, not as a curse. As such, it was meant to be treated with love and care, as we would care for a prized possession that we want to enjoy for decades to come. In addition to caring for our bodies for our own sakes, we also care for them for the sake of the Spirit who dwells within us.

Back to that sticking point. Think of a way you can engage this change a bit. The best modification would be one that stretches you a little in your habits and thinking without overstretching or pulling you apart. Think of some of the yoga stretches in which you have participated. The way you know you are really engaging your yoga practice is when you ride the edge of a stretch. There is some resistance, definitely some noticeable opening happening, but we never push so hard that we cause damage to ourselves. The same is true with changes in our life habits. We want to ride the edge of resistance. You will feel yourself being stretched and challenged but not pushed so hard as to tear yourself down.

Daily Exercise: Food Journal Revisited

Earlier we asked you to document the food you eat in a food journal. Remember and celebrate the changes you've already made. Now look at your habits again and see what new changes are possible. As always, give yourself grace. Eating is an area that can be two steps forward, one step backward. As long as the momentum is moving you forward into positive change, you are doing great!

This time as you consider your eating habits, emphasize a change that is concrete and specific. After all, change is incremental and slow. It is part of why diets that emphasize huge and quick changes do not tend to work as well as ones that emphasize slowly changing a lifestyle, changing the way you will live forever.

Think of just *one small change* that can have a big impact over time. Maybe it is cutting out a caffeinated drink at lunch, or maybe it's eliminating the sugar in your coffee. Write down a small change that will add up over time.

Once you have this change in mind, consider how to make it achievable and measurable. For example, I can say, "I'm going to quit sugar entirely!" But that will not work! It is not achievable, and not very measurable. What I can say is, "I am going to cut out one teaspoon of sugar in my coffee every weekday for one month." That way I am merely cutting one teaspoon (instead of two), giving myself a break on the weekends, and setting a goal of doing this for one month. Making the goal *achievable* means that you will have some success, instead of setting a goal that is unreasonable. You can always set a new, more challenging goal later, but it is best to start with a reasonable goal first. Making the goal *measurable* means that you can look back and see what you have done. Setting vague goals such as "I want to get healthy" are impossible to measure and do not set you up for success.

Reflection

Today's exercise seems easy at first, but when you start breaking down a goal into something more concrete and specific, then measurable and achievable, it can get complicated. There are a couple of reasons we encourage this sort of detailed work. First, it helps fight against the all-or-nothing (fight-or-flight) pattern that often happens with anxiety. Second, it is easier to measure progress when you have a clear marker for where you started and where you are going.

We used the example of food intake, but you could easily consider exercise too. So, instead of setting a goal of "I'm going to exercise," think through what form of exercise would work best for you and your schedule. A walk or run in the morning or evening may be more feasible than going to a gym. Once you have identified a specific form of exercise, get more detailed in terms of the time of day, how long you will exercise, and how often you will try to exercise over the course of a week.

Once you get these details set, think about whether walking or running a 5K every morning is a reasonable goal for you (for Dena it is definitely not!) or if you should make your goals smaller and more achievable. Remember too that building rest days into your schedule is also a way to care for your body. You may have set a measurable goal, but making it achievable will keep you from falling into the all-or-nothing trap.

Go back over what you wrote in your food journal for today's daily exercise. Check again whether the goal is concrete, specific, measurable, and achievable. Write that goal down here (and perhaps consider one more goal too).

CHAPTER 5: CHANGE

DAY 3

SHIFT IN COURSE

Read Exodus 16:1–12

At twilight you shall eat meat, and in the morning you shall have your fill of bread; then you shall know that I am the LORD your God. (v. 12)

THE BIBLE TALKS A LOT about the paths we take. While we are encouraged to walk on the right paths, paths of righteousness, the wonderful thing about God's grace is that no path we take is without God and his redeeming hand. In today's Scripture passage, the Israelites are complaining about the particular path they are on. They have just been set free from slavery to the Egyptians, but they are not content.

The new path frightens them. They are tired, hungry, and thirsty. Yet even as they complain and do not trust him, God mercifully provides for his people. He gives them the gift of bread in the morning and meat in the evening. But God instructs them to take only what they will eat in one day. Any surplus will spoil overnight. He wants to teach the Israelites a very important lesson on this particular path in the desert. He wants them to learn to trust their God to provide for them.

When the people do arrive at the edge of the promised land, get scared again, and refuse to take the land God promised to give them, he gives them even longer to learn what they need to know. For forty years they are forced to wander in the desert as their path takes them in circles. But even this was not in vain. After forty years of receiving manna in the morning and quail in the evening, daily trust in God's provision is ingrained in their souls.

The path was winding, but it still led to God. It reminds me of a labyrinth walk. If you are not familiar with labyrinth walking, the practice started at a cathedral at Chartres in France. Christians during this period of time were all encouraged to make a pilgrimage to the Holy Land, but then as now, many people could not afford the time away from family or from work or simply the cost that such a trip would entail. So as a sort of substitution, they would walk a circular, winding path etched into the floor of the cathedral. The idea of walking the labyrinth has led some modern churches to include stone or painted labyrinths on their property. In an attitude of prayer, people begin at the opening of the labyrinth and meditatively follow the path to the center. At the center many will stop and pray, then with prayer in each step, find their way out to the world again.

Whenever I have trod one of these carefully laid paths, I sometimes find myself frustrated by the circuitous route to the center. Just when I think I am getting close, the path swings out, away from the middle again. But this gives me a chance to remember that any step with God is not wasted. Our paths are often longer and more winding than we would wish, but they are still grace filled and used by God to get us where we need to be.

As you reflect on change this week, consider your movement through healing from anxiety. It so often takes longer and more effort than we want. But trust that God is with you, providing for you every step of the way—even when some of the steps feel like missteps, even when it feels like wandering. For there is one thing we know about our Shepherd: no matter how long or winding the path, the Good Shepherd always leads us home.

Daily Exercise: Labyrinth-Style Walk

Today you will take another walk, but it is not a move from point A to point B. This walk is made for wandering. If you have access to a labyrinth, it would be a wonderful tool to use. If not, you could do this walk in your own neighborhood or someplace nearby. Just allow yourself not to go straight from one place to another. Take the winding way. If walking is not an option, maybe you could try driving a new, less direct way to school or work or the store. Know that even if your travel is longer and less efficient, it will still bring you some goodness and grace.

Reflection

What did you notice on your walk or drive? We become so used to going a certain way, either driving the same way each day or walking the same path, that we miss new things along the route. Doing something new helps us think in different ways too. It is about changing patterns. So what did you notice on your new route?

_____
_____
_____
_____
_____
_____
_____
_____
_____
_____
_____
_____
_____
_____
_____
_____
_____
_____

CONVERSION OF THE MIND

Read Luke 19:1–10

Then Jesus said to him, "Today salvation has come to this house, because he too is a son of Abraham. For the Son of Man came to seek out and to save the lost." (vv. 9–10)

THE STORY OF ZACCHAEUS'S CONVERSION is one of my favorites. While initially it may not seem as dramatic as that of Paul's conversion story with its blinding light and booming voice of Jesus, the story is quite clear and to the point. Zacchaeus enters the story living one way and leaves by another way. Zacchaeus is not just a tax collector but a head tax collector, described as rich in a time and place when most people were poor. On a daily basis Zacchaeus likely made choices in which he took from other people so he could have more than he needed. Many of these choices probably involved abusing his power as a tax collector to oppress others. We do not know what led Zacchaeus into this pattern of behavior, but we can assume at some point he may have felt stuck in his role of a rich but despised member of society.

Although we do not have a word-for-word account of the conversation between Jesus and Zacchaeus, we know that Zacchaeus came down from the tree and welcomed Jesus into his home. What is obvious is the effect this encounter had on Zacchaeus. He is a new man. Instead of making the choice to take money from the already poor to line his pockets, he chooses to give half of his possessions to the poor and to make restitution to those he has wronged.

This story does not include the physical blindness and restoration of sight we read about with Paul, but Zacchaeus nonetheless sees with new eyes. That is what true repentance does: it gives us clear vision. Repentance is not just a moment of saying we are sorry, but it involves commitment to change course. God's grace gives us the ability to make the choice to leave the path we are on, turn, and live a different way. Our eyes see differently when we have been converted. Our mind makes different choices. This may be something that happens quickly as with Zacchaeus, but it is also something that continues to happen again and again over our lifetime.

While I do not necessarily consider my struggle with anxiety to be a sin, I do think it is an area of my life that is in the process of transformation. As a part of this transformation, I learn to see myself and the world with new eyes. My mind learns to make different choices. It is a condition that I am being saved from and a lostness in which I am continually being found.

As you look at the remaining weeks ahead in this journey of healing and restoration, know that by God's grace you, like Zacchaeus, have the power to begin thinking differently about yourself *and* the world. You have the power to allow that converted thinking to help you make new choices.

Sometimes the first change is letting our rigid minds soften enough to consider the possibility of changing course. It is important for us to remember that we are never stuck in our current patterns. We were designed to be moldable and changeable, as the potter works the clay. When we embrace this flexibility in thinking, a whole new range of possibilities opens up for us. Once this happens, God comes in and works with us to make a new creation. But in the end, we begin by making the choice to come down out of the tree.

Daily Exercise: Changing Your Mind

At the start of your day, plan how it is going to go. After you have set this plan, find five ways to change what you have decided. As you do this, know that you have the ability to choose what you do, not to have it chosen for you. Although many things in our lives are chosen for us, we do have a great deal of control over what we do next in a given day. Nonetheless, we often go through our days feeling little choice about what we do next. This feeling of lack of control can aggravate our anxiety. As you go through your day today, look for the choices in each situation. And remember, you do have the power to make a choice or to turn and make another.

Reflection

What did you choose today? Sometimes the choice is as simple (and difficult) as getting out of bed, but this still represents a choice— maybe an important first choice. Write about which choices were difficult. What choices surprised you? Maybe there is some aspect of your day that you dread, that always feels like a burden. Perhaps that is the place where you need to exercise some choice, to enact a change. If you feel comfortable, write about that choice or change.

_____

_____

_____

_____

_____

_____

_____

_____

_____

_____

_____

_____

_____

_____

_____

DAY 5

TRANSFORMATION

Read Genesis 32:22–32

Then the man said, "You shall no longer be called Jacob, but Israel, for you have striven with God and with humans, and have prevailed." (v. 28)

THIS PASSAGE DESCRIBES A BIG moment for Jacob, the man who entered the world by grabbing onto his twin's heel. Jacob tricked his own hungry brother into giving him his birthright and later tricked his blind father into giving him the blessing that rightfully belonged to the eldest, Esau. Jacob was a trickster among tricksters. In today's passage Jacob comes to a point of reckoning. Rich in possessions and descendants, he has finally left the home of his father-in-law and is traveling back to the land of his birth, his homeland. This return home confronts Jacob with a decision: What kind of person will he be from this point on? Will he be the swindler of his youth, ever struggling with his older brother? Will he be the manipulator he was with his father-in-law? Will he be someone entirely new?

One night along this journey home, Jacob wrestles with an unknown stranger, and in so doing, he wrestles with his past and with his future. As the day dawns, two remarkable things happen. First, the heavenly stranger touches Jacob's hip, injuring him to the point that he will walk with a limp. Second, the stranger gives him a new name. Every day from this point on Jacob—Israel— will remember this night. Every day going forward he will not be the same. He will be blessed and reconciled, but he will walk with a limp as a reminder of his transformation.

We ask you to think of today as a touchstone moment in your

transformation. We will not ask you to wrestle with anyone, for we imagine that you have wrestled with many things already. But we do ask you to think of this as the day you are blessed with a new name. Before this day, you may have had many names for yourself. Some of these may be negative names you have given to yourself. Some may be names that were given to you by parents or teachers years ago. Some may be names given by loved ones in the present.

But today is a turning point. Every day can be a turning point, but we ask that you think of today as one of those points to which you will look back and say, "Before I was like this and after, like that."

As you come to think of yourself in a different way, not necessarily with a new name that others will know, be mindful of the limp. That limp is not a reminder that it "never gets better" (although that is what our negative thinking patterns will tell us sometimes). The limp is a reminder that we will always struggle a bit. It is a reminder of our humanity in the middle of our strength. Even Jesus, after the resurrection, retained the wounds in his hands, feet, and side.

Daily Exercise: My New Name

Find fifteen to twenty minutes today for a time of quiet, uninterrupted prayer. This should be a time where you can find stillness and be able to listen. You may notice the noise and worry of your mind, but then return to the presence of your breath. Know that God is with you in the silence.

If you have difficulty finding quiet stillness, listen to the voice of Jesus as he says to the storms, "Peace, be still." Allow this to be a phrase you imagine hearing Jesus say to you. "Peace, be still."

Once you find the quiet, just sit and listen. Listen to what God might be saying to you. Listen to what may be your new name. Listen for what God might want you to know. Perhaps the message is for you to know God is with you. Maybe you need to see yourself as the child of God you already are. Perhaps you need to say, "God is with me, even in the deep waters." It may be you need to remind yourself of God's grace for you and for everyone.

After you have found that word or name for yourself, take a moment more to breathe, breathing in God's peace, breathing out your thanks to God. Sit for another minute or two, then slowly move out of this time and into the rest of your day.

Reflection

What is the name or message you heard during the exercise? Write about your quiet time of listening today.

If you read further in the story of Jacob and Esau, you find that as Jacob goes to meet Esau, he is afraid. He is afraid his brother will be angry because of Jacob's past treachery, but when they finally do meet, Esau welcomes Jacob with an embrace. Jacob had sent many gifts ahead, hoping to gain Esau's mercy, but Esau tells his brother he has plenty—Jacob should keep his gifts. Jacob entreats his brother to accept the gifts, "For truly to see your face is like seeing the face of God—since you have received me with such favor" (Gen. 33:10).

The face of God often surprises us. I pray you heard God's welcoming voice for you during this exercise, and that like Jacob you saw his face of favor. Consider writing about what you heard in your time of listening.

_____

_____

_____

_____

_____

_____

_____

_____

CHAPTER 5: CHANGE

DAY 6

CONVERSION

Read Luke 17:11–19

*Then [Jesus] said to him, "Get up and go on your way;
your faith has made you well." (v. 19)*

JESUS'S WORDS TO THE LEPER that his faith had made him well can
be difficult for those with anxiety to process. It is hard because
it seems to us that anxiety and faith are opposites. If we have
faith, then we will not worry, right? And this can lead us to think,
Maybe I don't have faith.

We tend to have a very point-in-time view of salvation and faith.
You either believe or you do not believe. At one point you were
unsaved, and now you are saved. But Christians have not always
looked at their relationship with God in this clearly defined way.
For most of Christian history, people have recognized that a walk
with God has a beginning, but then it often winds its way closer to
and farther away from him—like the labyrinth. Like the Israelites
wandering in the wilderness, God's people go through times of
fidelity and times of turning away.

Our own times of wandering are part of our walk with God.
Sometimes we grumble. Sometimes we worry. Sometimes we wonder why. Sometimes we are anxious, and sometimes we harbor a
deep fear that our anxiety is a sign that we are *not* God's.

In today's reading, we have the healing of ten lepers. And as
you may remember, only one of them returned to thank Jesus for
the healing. And that one was a Samaritan. A quick note on being
a Samaritan in the New Testament: you were not fully of God.
You were likely of mixed ethnic and religious heritage. You did
not belong with the Jews and were not exactly a Gentile either.

And like most people who do not "fit," you would have felt your status as an outsider. But it was the outsider who returned to thank Jesus; the insiders, who typically feel more entitled to their healings, never thanked Jesus.

Sometimes it is when we know what it is like to feel outside, to feel broken in some way, that we are most grateful for God's provision and healing. In the end, we all know that we do not *deserve* God's grace. But often it is one who is outside who is acutely aware of the *generosity* of God toward all of us. And that our proper response is one of thanks.

For many of us this path is one from feeling apart and outside toward a closeness and intimacy with God. But hearing words such as Jesus saying, "Your faith has made you well" can sound more like it has been *our* steps and *our* effort that gets us to this point-in-time conversion or healing.

But is that the only way to read it? There are so many stories in the Hebrew Scriptures and New Testament where belief or faith does not lead to immediate change. There are many places where change takes time and much wandering in our wildernesses. There is a process and ongoing discipleship to our faith. Odds are that becoming truly well, being restored to a community and finding a sense of belonging there, was probably a process for this newly healed Samaritan leper.

And working through our anxiety is a process also.

Whereas we would love for our healing from anxiety to be a point-in-time event, it rarely works that way. But the gift is that the long, winding journey we take with God can give us a greater experience of gratitude toward God. If you have dealt with feelings of being outside the norm of your faith community because of your struggle with anxiety, then you will have a greater appreciation for God's welcome of us as beloved children. When you come face-to-face with your limits and places of brokenness, you will have a greater awareness of the generosity of God's abundant grace. Though our struggle with anxiety is often frustrating, it can serve to highlight the miracle of God's love weaving itself through the ups and downs of our lives.

Daily Exercise: Writing About Conversion and Change

Take a few moments today to ponder changes that God has already brought to you. Maybe it is noting some small change in your anxiety, or it could be remembering back to the beginning of your journey with God. John Wesley writes about a moment when his heart was "strangely warmed," a time when he felt great assurance of God's love for him. Perhaps you also have had times when you were assured of God's love, aware of God's presence, or felt some new knowledge of God's love for you and others. Write prayerfully about a time or multiple times when you felt God's love and presence with you.

Reflection

There is some interesting research that is quite useful in helping people change. Behavioral scientists doing research on addiction identified two important things about the process of change:

1. Change is a process of action, maintenance, failing, and trying again.
2. There are some distinct steps to changing and to have successful change.[12]

What changes do you feel like you have already made and how do you think you can maintain them? Some will find people to whom they can be accountable. Others will set goals to keep themselves motivated.

Remember that relapse is a part of recovery. This means that when (not if) you fail, consider what may have led to the relapse. Adjust your plan for recovery so you can avoid a similar situation in the future. Resist the temptation to tell yourself that you will always fail.

God calls us to respond in thanks for the healing that has already happened and to continue moving toward healing, even though the journey may have detours and bumps along the way. In your plan for maintenance, consider who is there to support you. What will help you remember to "choose healthy"? What do you need to avoid that does not help? What small steps have made a big difference?

_____

_____

_____

_____

_____

_____

_____

_____

_____

_____

_____

_____

_____

_____

_____

_____

_____

_____

_____

_____

CHANGING OUR COMMUNITIES
(OR HOW WE INTERACT WITH THEM)

Read 1 Thessalonians 5:1–5

For you are all children of light and children of the day;
we are not of the night or of darkness. (v. 5)

I REMEMBER HAVING THIS VERSE in 1 Thessalonians 5 drilled into me as a young college student. The message was clear: if you want to be a certain kind of person, then surround yourself with people who support you being that person. If my goal was to live my life as a clean-cut, God-seeking young woman, then I needed to surround myself with people who supported that. Our leaders made it clear to us that this support system did not include partying friends or boyfriends who pushed for physical intimacy. As simplistic as this teaching sounds, there is a lot of truth to the idea. The people who are around us have a big influence on our life. (Just try going on a diet and then having dinner out with people who order large platters of fried cheese appetizers!)

Today we are going to think about the people in your daily life and the impact they may be having on your anxiety recovery. This is tricky because we can choose to surround ourselves with some people, such as friends and church family, but we cannot choose *not* to have some people in our lives—like family or coworkers. All these people, chosen or not, are tightly woven into the fabric of who we are.

But whether we have chosen the people in our life or not, *we always have a choice in how we will interact with them.* This is important, because certain people are helpful to our anxiety recovery and certain people are not. So what do we do about this?

An obvious first answer is to increase our connectedness with those people in our lives who help us be healthy. As we read in 1 Thessalonians, God desires for us to be children of the light. If there are friends, family members, or coworkers who lighten up your life, then make an effort to be with them. Arrange a lunch date, join a Bible study, or just pick up the phone and contact these light bringers. If you do not have such a group of people, find them! Find a good church that has small group programs and sign up to participate in one. Sure, it is a risk, but it could pay big dividends when you develop relationships of support that bless your life.

What about people who do not understand our anxiety struggles and even aggravate them? When someone is consistently a dark cloud in your life, it is time to create some distance. If it is a voluntary relationship, such as a friendship or church connection, then start by being less available. Limit the time and the contexts in which you are with them. Do not feel guilty about making this space. You may worry that it is not the right time to set boundaries since your friend might need you. As Thessalonians reminds us, the time is now. If you do not step up and stand up for yourself, then you will come to the end of your life and realize you never made the time to live as your best, most vibrant self. Wake up and choose to be in relationships that build up instead of tear down.

You may wonder how you can make this choice for healthy relationships when the relationship is not so voluntary. You cannot just walk away from a difficult in-law or a problem child. What is a child of light to do? Again, even though you may not feel free to walk away from difficult relationships, you can choose how you will allow yourself to be treated. You do not have to say yes to every family gathering, and you can refuse to join negative patterns of behavior in your family when you are together. This is not easy. It may take some time, therapeutic support, and lots of practice. A good resource is the book *Boundaries* by Henry Cloud and John Townsend.

We know that making changes to and within our relationships is not easy. This may be some of the hardest but most necessary work you do in your anxiety recovery. For now, just trust that it is important. *Because you are important.* God's desire is for you to know love and joy and hope, and sometimes these things come to us most clearly through human hands. Set yourself up to receive these good gifts by surrounding yourself with people who can give them to you. It will not always be easy, but in the end it will definitely be worth it.

Daily Exercise: Relationship Pictograph

Take a page of paper and draw circles around yourself to represent the friends and family in your life. You can use the sample below:

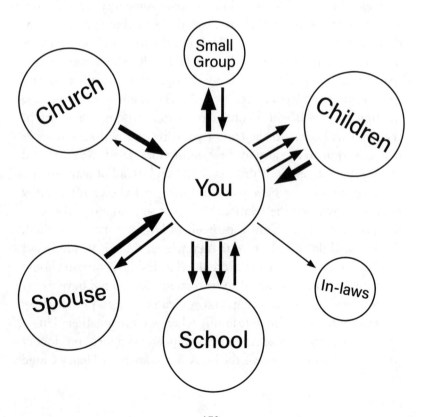

Draw little arrows to represent whether energy and support move from this person toward you or from you toward them. You can even make the lines thicker or thinner depending on how much energy seems to flow in that direction. There may be many instances when arrows go both ways. Note if this person is helpful in your recovery from anxiety or if this is a person who raises your stress level and aggravates your anxiety.

Reflection

Take a second look at your relationship pictograph. Note the relationships that show a good, healthy presence in your life. Consider ways you can encourage these relationships. Then note those relationships that seem to be continuous stressors for you and think of some ways to distance yourself. Take steps to create healthy boundaries to protect yourself from complicated family relationships and their negative impact.

Remember that when we are anxious or overwhelmed, we make choices that do not feel like a choice. We say things like, "Well, I have to" or, "No one else will do it if I don't."

Think about how much energy is moving in and out of you and these relationships. Write about changes you may need to make.

_____

_____

_____

_____

_____

_____

_____

_____

_____

_____

_____

_____

_____

CHAPTER 5 REVIEW

Where is the place you see the most change in yourself?

What changes seem to be the hardest to make?

Why might this be so?

What is one small change that you can make in this difficult area?

If change is a process, where are you in that journey?

How is your name or identity changing?

How can you go ahead and start claiming your new identity?

Change is hard. We hope that you have heard throughout this chapter a message of hope but also some very practical steps to making changes. In addition, and most importantly, remember that our God is full of grace, forgiveness, and love for us. When you are talking to yourself about change and listening for God's voice inside you and in those around you, listen for that voice of love and encouragement, not of judgment and fear.

CHAPTER 6

SPIRIT

DAY 1

LETTING GO OF CONTROL

Read Job 38:4-18

Have you commanded the morning since your days began,
and caused the dawn to know its place? (v. 12)

WHO IS REALLY IN CONTROL? Me or God?

The theme of this week is tackling some of the spiritual challenges that emerge with anxiety. One of these challenges is our need for control, which is a root cause of anxiety.

Take my phobia of airplane travel. Most of my fear of flying comes from the sensation of being trapped in a situation I have little control over. If I could fly the plane or even sit in the cockpit and pepper the pilot with questions and advice, my emotions would be much more at ease. I pray for the Holy Spirit to be with me before I fly. I utter all sorts of words that may or may not sound like prayers to some, but every time I say, "Jesus," believe me, I am praying about the turbulence that I cannot control.

Having a sense of control and power in our lives is not in itself a bad thing. The problems come when we try to control things that are either beyond our control or have no need of our influence. Take breathing. We may worry we are not getting a good breath or that our breath will end. But in reality, our breathing happens whether we choose it or not. We can exert control over the breath to deepen it or lengthen it, but the act of inhaling and exhaling happens on its own as a function of our autonomic (or automatic) nervous system. If you have ever known a child who threatens to hold their breath until they die, you know what happens. They might pass out, but then their breath will start up again by itself.

So it goes with so many things we worry about—events that

are either beyond our control (the problems and actions of other people) or have no need for us to control them. The beauty of nature—a mountain range, a deep canyon, the ocean, or simply the sun rising—reminds us of God's ultimate control and the preciousness of that truth. The sun rises every day whether we worry about it or not. The truth is that although we may have an illusion of control in our life, we have much less power than we think. This is good news, because there is One who does have ultimate control in this world. And the One with this privilege and responsibility is even more trustworthy than we are. This news is a balm for our spirits, because it lets our spirits rest in the One who set the stars in the sky and calls the sun to rise.

When we can join Job, learning to trust the Holy Spirit to handle the sunrise, the movement of the earth, our breath, and even the problems of our loved ones, we can relax into our role as a person on the journey instead of the one flying the plane.

Daily Exercise: Releasing the Breath

Today you will practice a reverse breathing exercise. Instead of being intentional about your breath or trying to manipulate it, you are just going to let it be. Make no effort to change it in any way. Just observe that you inhale and exhale successfully over and over.

Find your comfortable breathing position, but this time just observe your breathing. Listen to the breath flow in and out of your body. You may even have a sensation not of breathing but of being breathed. After a few minutes of resting in this place of natural breath, say a prayer of thanks for all that God controls and maintains in your life. As you ease back into your day, take with you the knowledge of God's providence and care.

Reflection

It is very hard for us to grasp and practice the reality of God's control. Most of us have the illusion of being in control ourselves. From the time we are toddlers, we say no. As young children we press a button on a toy, and when it makes a noise, our control of it makes us smile. As adolescents, we test the limits of our control. Yet, as we grow older, we begin to feel those limits more acutely. Sometimes our awareness of our limited control comes when we watch loved ones suffer, as we face illnesses of our own, as we parent children with their own notions of control, as we lose relationships and even marriages to circumstances beyond our ability to fix or manage.

Recognizing the limits of our control is part of having good boundaries. Sometimes our greatest challenge is seeing what is our responsibility, what is someone else's, and what is ultimately God's to manage.

Today has been about noticing what happens, even when we are not trying. Think of events that happen without you. These may be large or small, with the help of human hands (perhaps a meal being provided), or without anyone else's intervention at all. List some of the signs of God's provision and sustenance to you. Maybe include on the list some of the people and circumstances about which you worry and that you can release, at least for a moment, to God.

_____

_____

_____

_____

_____

_____

_____

_____

_____

_____

_____

_____

_____

_____

_____

STRENGTH FOR THE JOURNEY

Read 1 Kings 19:1–18

He looked, and there at his head was a cake baked on hot stones, and a jar of water. He ate and drank, and lay down again. The angel of the LORD came a second time, touched him, and said, "Get up and eat, otherwise the journey will be too much for you." (vv. 6–7)

SEVERAL WEEKS AGO WE CONSIDERED this passage in the context of the need to start moving. Spurred on by stress hormones and the fight-or-flight response, Elijah moved away from the threat that Queen Jezebel posed. But what happened after Elijah quit running? He settled underneath a broom tree and simply stopped, spent from the effort, exhausted from the threats to his life, weary in his very bones.

Many people think what is depicted here is a highly esteemed prophet experiencing depression. As Elijah sank to the ground, so did his spirit. For many of us who have endured chronic stressors, we reach the point where we have no ability to move forward. Depression brings not only a low mood, but body aches, slow movements, low appetite, and a deep physical, mental, and spiritual exhaustion. Research indicates there may well be a link between depression as an illness and autoimmune disorders and inflammatory illnesses.[13] Our brains, our bodies, and our spirits are tired, and we feel chronically stressed, overwhelmed, and beaten.

Elijah had just participated in a great and wonderful showing of God's power, and then he ran, fled, and stopped, unable to move on. He even said out loud, as many people in the depths of depression have thought, "Just let me die here."

Perhaps he was tired. Maybe he was scared. What we know for certain is he did not wish to move. And that is when the angel arrived. The angel did not offer Elijah words. What he offered was sustenance, bodily nourishment. It looked like communion as the Christian church understands it. The bread and wine offered in the New Testament by Jesus at the Lord's Supper was not a special meal. It didn't have to be flown in from a foreign land. Bread and wine were the staples of the people. Elijah was given the basics, what was needed to get him a little bit further. Bread and drink.

Another surprising and wonderfully honest portion of this passage is that even after eating, Elijah still could not go on. This is sometimes true for many of us. Our first effort, or the first efforts of those who love us, is not enough. Not giving up on Elijah, God sent the angel again. God did not offer a new intervention. It was still the basics: bread and drink. And this time, Elijah continued on his journey.

Daily Exercise: Mindful Eating

Could you tell someone what you ate yesterday? Were bread and wine on the menu? Most of us cannot say, without some intense thought, what we had for breakfast, lunch, and dinner yesterday. We often look at food as just something to fill us for the moment, not paying close attention to what we eat and drink. An activity Jason often uses in teaching mindfulness is called mindful eating.

To try this today, pick one meal or even one snack and pay attention to every part of the process of eating. First, note how the food feels in your hand or the way unwrapping or peeling feels to you. Notice the smells associated with the food as you bring it closer to you. Notice the temperature of the food. After noticing the texture, smell, and other qualities of the food, break off one small piece. Notice how your mouth prepares to receive the food, the way muscles move and salivary glands function to prepare you for the food. Allow the food to sit in your mouth for just a minute so you fully taste it, noticing the feel of it inside your mouth. When you are ready, begin to chew, slowly and deliberately. Notice how your mouth and throat prepare to swallow. As you swallow, notice all the changes in your mouth and throat. Practice this way of eating with the rest of your meal or snack, taking time with the activity, noticing all aspects—not judging the actions or food but just noticing them and being thankful for all the nourishment God provides for us in so many forms.

Reflection

Where do you find God providing sustenance for your body and spirit? Sometimes it is food and drink, as it was for Elijah, but other times it is the comfort of a bed, the warm water of a shower or bath, the embrace of a loved one. Sometimes these are reminders to stop, to notice the seemingly small supports around you. Write down where you find strength, physically and spiritually, for your journey. Be as specific as you can. For example, instead of writing "bread," write about the biscuits your aunt used to make or the feel of that warm roll in your hand, tearing off just a bit from the crusty exterior and noticing the soft interior.

DAY 3

RIDING THE WAVES OF LIFE

Read Isaiah 43:1–3

*When you pass through the waters, I will be with you;
and through the rivers, they shall not overwhelm you;
when you walk through the fire you shall not be burned,
and the flame shall not consume you. (v. 2)*

WATER IS A MAJOR IMAGE in the Old Testament. But the thing about these waters is they usually represent much more than ordinary H_2O. The waters we read about often represent the waters of chaos, a dark destructive force that ancient people feared. This is why it is so powerful that God brought order and control to the waters at creation, that God promised never to let the waters rage in destruction again after the flood, that God separated the waters to bring the Israelites to freedom, and that God reminds us here in Isaiah that the waters—though they threaten—will not take his people under their swirling depths.

God does not say that we will never have to enter the waters or deal with their force again. He does say that he will be with us and will not let the waters overwhelm us. It is as if God is helping us become water riders so we can survive and even thrive with the chaotic forces at play in our lives.

This verse in Isaiah reminds me of the first time my daughter played in the ocean. She waded out into the surf of the Atlantic only to be knocked off-balance time and time again by the waves crashing around her little legs. She looked at me tearfully and cried, "Mommy, make the waves stop!" I walked closer to her and said, "Honey, I can't make the waves stop, but I can teach you to play in them."

The waves in our life will never stop. Our world is full of movement, and some of it feels like a crashing wave that will knock us off our feet and drag us under. But we were created to be above the waves. If we can learn to watch them and to ride them, they become a force that can propel us forward instead of threatening to drown us with their power.

The little girl that once cried in the Atlantic waves is bigger now, and she has learned how to read the ocean's waves. She no longer tries to plant her little legs and resist their force, but instead she swims and rides the movement of the waves. At the end of the day when she is tired, she has learned to simply paddle a little deeper, turn on her back, and float.

Daily Exercise: Cat/Cow

Today we will practice the simple yoga move of a cat/cow flow. Once we find the flow of breath and movements in these two poses, they will simulate the waves we want to learn to ride.

Wear comfortable clothing and find a place on the floor or bed where you feel comfortable getting on your hands and knees. When you are ready, come to a hands-and-knees, table-like position on the ground. Take a moment to get in touch with the steady flow of your breath. After a few rounds of breath, begin to link the flow of your body with the rhythm of your breath. On an inhalation, drop your belly toward the ground, tuck your tailbone up, and lift your head and heart toward the sky. Keep your arms basically straight, connected to the ground, and keep your body stable with your shoulders over your hands and your hips over your knees. The spine is what finds the most movement, with head and heart opening. Next, on your exhalation, tuck your chin to your chest, drop your tailbone toward the ground, and lift the middle of your back toward the sky. Your form will resemble an angry cat. Continue moving through these two positions with the rhythm of your breath. Inhalation will find you in a cow position with your belly sunk down and back arched in a backbend.

Exhalation will bring you to the hissing cat form. Ride the wave of breath and the wave of your body's movements for a few minutes. Enjoy the ebb and flow of your movements as you link them with the ebb and flow of the breath. Know that you have the power to be a wave rider. If thoughts come to your mind while in this flow, simply ride their coming and going as well.

When you are ready to be finished, come back to your hands and knees and notice how your body and mind feel after this flow. You can come back to this flow of movement anytime you need it.

Reflection

Sometimes our actions make situations worse instead of better. Sometimes our anxiety takes hold and we act in ways that further complicate the situation. This often happens because we move into the anxious all-or-nothing mode of thinking and cannot think creatively about a response . . . or about the option of just waiting and watching.

Sometime today choose to take a deep breath and wait. If you choose to act, do so in a way that is less anxious, less reactive, and more intentional and thoughtful. This is like riding the wave, paddling out a bit, and floating.

Write about this time today.

_____

_____

_____

_____

_____

_____

_____

_____

_____

_____

_____

DAY 4

LEARNING TO TRUST

Read Mark 4:35–41

*He said to them, "Why are you afraid? Have you still no
faith?" (v. 40)*

I HAVE SO MUCH COMPASSION for the disciples in this passage.
They are riding along in their boat when a great storm arises. The
wind whips and the waves beat against their small craft. As sea
spray drenches their faces and water pools at their feet, fear rises
in their hearts. Fear tells them that the winds will not stop. Fear
shouts that the waves will grow bigger. Fear says their boat will
be overturned and overtaken by the chaotic deep.

As fear wells up like a wave in the disciples, they notice that
one among them is not studying the stormy sea with furrowed
brow. Their teacher, Jesus, is sleeping in the stern of the boat.
They rouse their leader and friend and ask, "Do you not care that
we are perishing?"

The disciples could have meant this question in one of two
ways. The first is belief that Jesus was capable of solving their
problem but confusion that he appeared unconcerned about doing
so. The second is perplexity that Jesus did not seem to care that
he was about to lose his own life in this storm. Was he not afraid
for himself? It certainly appeared that all of them, Jesus included,
were about to perish.

Whatever the disciples meant, Jesus's response surprised them.
When they woke him up, Jesus rebuked the wind and spoke peace
to the sea, and soon all was calm again. Then he turned to the
disciples and asked them, "Why are you afraid? Have you still no
faith?"

Jesus's questions have troubled me in my spiritual life. Many use his words as a justification for beating people up for their fear. "Why are you afraid?" they ask. "Have you no faith?" The questions are asked with more condemnation than compassion. Soon we wonder for ourselves. *Why am I so afraid? Is my faith so weak? Is my fear a sin? Am I failing at following God?*

Then I come back to Jesus. God's Word tells us Jesus asks them, "Why are you afraid?" It does not say he rebukes the disciples. That language is used for the waves. He does not chastise the disciples as he does the raging waters. His question implies what I ask my frightened child: "Didn't you know I would come for you?" The question comes not from anger but from frustration and sadness that the one you love has not yet learned to trust your ability and commitment to care for them. The question emerges out of a deep concern that your loved one has missed an essential quality about your character and the relationship that you share together.

The disciples had missed this. They had missed that Jesus was so powerful that even the winds and sea obeyed him. They had also missed that he could be trusted to care for them and would never let them be overtaken by the deep.

I miss this too. The fear comes in, and the tears well up. All I can see are the waves. I miss that my Savior is resting close by. I miss that I am cared for and loved and will never face the waves alone.

Rather than calling this a sin to be condemned, maybe it is just a part of our human condition that needs saving. We are not left to our own fear because we have a Savior who speaks peace to us. God reminds us that Jesus is Immanuel, God with us. May we let this good news fill our spirits and bring us awe.

Daily Exercise: Praying Scripture

Find a quiet place where you can be uninterrupted for ten minutes. Bring yourself to a centered place in mind and body. We will introduce a Scripture prayer based on verse 41 from our reading: "Who is this whom the sea and wind obey?" Not only is breathing and praying Scripture a centering practice, but this particular prayer is designed to let us explore our relationship with Jesus. Eventually this prayer will heal our battered spirts and draw us closer to Jesus.

After you steady your breath, begin repeating this prayer over and over to yourself. You may want to link it to your breath as with the breath prayer by saying "Who is this" on the inhalation and then "whom the sea and wind obey" on the exhalation. Let these words sink into your soul. If thoughts and ideas come to you as you breathe, feel free to ponder the question, but do not feel as if you have to actually answer the question. Let the repeating of the question be enough for now. Continue breathing and praying in this way, feeling a rhythm with body and spirit. After several minutes have passed, allow the prayer to fall away and return to the breath. Notice if your mind and body feel different than when you started. When you come to an anxious moment later today, feel free to return to the prayer to remind yourself of Christ's presence and action in your life.

Reflection

We are often afraid to ask the difficult questions. Sometimes we are afraid to utter them to one another. We are certainly afraid at times to ask God, "Where are you?" or, "Don't you care that I am about to drown?"

Notice that in the daily activity you are not asked to reassure yourself of an answer to the question, "Who is this?" It is enough to ask the question and then simply sit with God. Today is the day where we focus on our minds, and that includes our fear. Sometimes that includes the ultimate fear that we are alone, that God is not with us after all.

Today write down your questions. Consider your ultimate question and write it down, knowing you do not have to have the answer. Trying to have the answer is just one more way we try to control God. Allow God to have the question you write down, praying as you write.

_____

_____

_____

_____

_____

_____

_____

_____

_____

_____

_____

_____

_____

_____

_____

_____

_____

_____

_____

_____

_____

_____

_____

_____

_____

_____

_____

_____

_____

DAY 5

WADE IN THE WATERS

Read Matthew 3:13-17

And when Jesus had been baptized, just as he came up from the water, suddenly the heavens were opened to him and he saw the Spirit of God descending like a dove and alighting on him. (v. 16)

WATER. UP UNTIL TODAY, WE have written about an ominous churning of the waters and the waves. There is also the threat of what lies underneath the surface of the chaotic, murky depths. But today, we consider the water of baptism: soothing, healing waters. This is water as the path to redemption. This is water that shows us God loves us and accepts us. This is the water by which we become part of a larger community.

In most Christian churches and throughout Christian history, the rite of baptism has been a way of initiation into the Christian community. Although some of the imagery is about the washing away of sin, much of the water imagery has to do with change that is about more than becoming clean.

Think about the way God brings the beauty of creation out of the murky deep. Then God delivers Noah and recreates the world through the waters of the great flood. The children of Israel move through the waters of the Red Sea, parted by God's power through his servant Moses. On one side of the Red Sea the people were slaves; on the other side they were moving toward a new life in a promised land.

In the New Testament, we are introduced to baptism through John the Baptist, one who preached repentance, from the Greek word *metanoia*, which means to turn from one thing to something new. You can hear the echoes of the Old Testament in Matthew 3, echoes of an exodus from one life to another.

Much of the imagery in the New Testament looks at baptism as a death and resurrection, becoming a new creation. The earliest Christian traditions baptized once a year, always on Easter after a long period of preparation for the candidates. The resurrection of Jesus was paired with the new life that these converts had chosen.

Even though we often see baptism as something we do, the Bible is clear that the giving of grace is ultimately God's act for us. Grace is not something we do for ourselves. Salvation is a gift, not anything we could ever merit or earn. If God's grace were something we had to earn, something we had to be "good enough" to receive, this would certainly be cause for a great deal of anxiety. It would lead us to wonder whether we are good enough or have done enough—and, of course, the answer will always be no. Ultimately, our inability would overwhelm us, and we would never understand God's abundant love for us.

If some of our anxiety is about our control versus God's control, about being good enough, then a corrective to this thinking may be to "enter the water." Although traditions vary on baptizing more than once, many traditions allow other ways you can "touch the water" to remember and to participate again in God's grace. This is why many Catholic churches keep a small bowl of baptismal water at the entrance of the church.

Floating is another way to reflect on the healing and soothing nature of water. You enter a body of water and allow yourself to rest on and in the water. In such a moment you can physically feel the water surround you, holding you, enveloping you. You float not of your own effort. The water sustains you. Similarly, God's sustaining grace comes not by your own effort.

Daily Exercise: Touching Water

Take some time today to be in contact with water in a purposeful and meditative way. Maybe you have the opportunity to actually enter a pool or lake and spend some time floating. If you are able to float, release yourself to that action, allowing yourself to be held up and buoyed by the water around you. If this is not possible, then draw yourself a nice full bath. If you do not have access to a bathtub, then use a sink full of water and practice this activity by letting your hand be the agent of your body to enter the water. As you lie in the pool or bath or drop your hand into the filled sink, release yourself to the support of the water around you. Let your arms and hands be held up by the strength of all that surrounds you. Consciously make the choice to let go of your own weight and effort, letting yourself be held by this other. If floating is difficult for you, do not be angry at yourself or feel you are failing. Just feel the water as it surrounds all of you, knowing this body of water is larger than you, just as God is so much larger than you. As you are held and caressed by the water, "enter the water" more and more. Release into this pool of grace your worries, your need for control, your faults and weaknesses, all that you are holding on to. Enjoy the feel of the water moving over you, cleansing you of all that needs to be washed away. After a period of time, prepare to reenter your day. As you leave the water, feel free to leave behind all that you needed to release to God. Give thanks for this sacred gift of water that gives us life and health each day.

Reflection

Although we typically think of baptism as an action we take, it is a sign of God's grace given *to* us, not taken *by* us. Many times we think of actions we take to make change happen, but there are also profound moments when change is happening apart from our own actions. Sometimes this change is quite difficult and is accompanied by what feels like destructive forces. At other times, these changes come quietly but with profound consequences for our lives.

Write down a change you are aware of that is not something you have done but is something God has brought to you. Ideally, this is a good and welcome change, but we may also need to think of a change we did not choose. These changes are the ones where we look for God to bring good out of evil, to bring new life out of what feels like death.

In all of this, we need to remember the limits of our control and the provision of God. Write a few sentences about a time when you found that change happened and God provided a way through.

_____

_____

_____

_____

_____

_____

_____

_____

_____

_____

_____

_____

_____

_____

_____

_____

_____

_____

_____

_____

_____

_____

_____

WHERE IS GOD WHEN TIMES ARE HARD?

Read Matthew 8:23–27

And they went and woke him up, saying, "Lord, save us! We are perishing!" (v. 25)

TODAY WE LOOK AGAIN AT the passage where Jesus calms the storm, but this time we focus on the first and in many ways harder half of this passage. The disciples had spent many moments, possibly even hours, in hard, dangerous, and life-threatening storms. This is only one of many "storms" the disciples weathered with Jesus. Herein lies a truth we do not always like to face about our faith. Following Jesus doesn't mean we get a pass on suffering. Just the opposite. Jesus tells us if we follow him, we will suffer and struggle (John 16:33).

A life of faith is not all "Victory in Jesus," though many people will tell us it should be. The hard truth is we will suffer many storms in life before the final victory is won. The wind will blow and the waves will rage. We will wonder if we are about to be overcome by it all. It will seem as if God does not know or care about our storm. He will remain silent.

Just when we think we cannot take another gust of wind or another drop of water, the storm will end. It may take forty days and forty nights, but eventually the storm will end. We will stand, rain soaked, beaten down, and weathered to the bone. But we will be there, and life will go on.

I cannot explain why this is so. People have written a multitude of books on the "problem of evil"—the problem of believing in an all-good, all-powerful God in a world full of pain and suffering. When I question where God is when I suffer, I often remember God asking Job where he was when the Word created the world. I do not have to understand it all. I hold on to the thought that all the while God is with me—even if it seems that my Beloved is sleeping while I am tossed upon the deep, dark sea.

I pray you have this comfort as well, to know God is with you in the storm even when it does not seem so. To know that even though today may be difficult, someday it will end. The winds will cease, the waves will calm, and peace will reign again. The ultimate reality is that Jesus does reign. Sometimes we just have to weather a storm or two in the meantime.

Daily Exercise: "Be Still" Meditation

Find a quiet place where you will be uninterrupted for ten minutes. You will recite a layered breath prayer using the verse "Be still, and know that I am God" (Ps. 46:10). After you have become settled and found your steady breath, pray "Be still, and know that I am God" in rhythm with your breath. After a few steady belly breaths, repeat the phrase "Be still, and know that I am." After a few more breaths, recite the verse "Be still, and know." Again, after a few breaths recite "Be still." Finally, after several breaths repeat the single word "Be." After soaking in this word for a few breaths, repeat the process back out again. Repeat the words "Be still." Then after a few breaths recite "Be still, and know." Then breathe the words "Be still, and know that I am." And finally recall with the breath the words "Be still, and know that I am God." Let yourself breathe in this truth for a few minutes and then release the thought meditation. After another moment, you can release back to a normal pattern of breathing. Take a moment to be aware of any differences in how you feel at the end of this meditation. Know that you can use it again anytime you wish.

Reflection

How is God all good, all powerful, and all loving when there is evil in the world? Scholars and philosophers like to call this seeming contradiction the "problem of evil." Some say God is the author of evil because in the end it helps us grow spiritually. Some say that God limits his own power by giving us free will. While this may explain some of the evil we do to others and that has been done to us, it does not necessarily explain terrible natural evils such as earthquakes, tsunamis, and hurricanes.

With all the words used to resolve this problem, I can tell you from having sat with many people in the midst of death and tragedy that there are no words that can explain away pain. In the midst of death and suffering, the loss of children and parents, the pain of betrayal by loved ones, sometimes there can only be the shedding of tears.

As a person of faith and someone who thinks about managing anxiety, I consider the best response to often be no response at all. It is our worry that leads us to search for an explanation for tragedy, but there is no good explanation. For the Christian, these are Good Friday moments—moments where we experience the death of Jesus and find *God is suffering with us.* This is relationship with God.

In your response today, think of a time not when God "fixed" the suffering but when you felt his presence in the midst of the suffering. Perhaps you can think of a time when you felt God's absence instead. The "dark night of the soul" is also a part of our journey of faith. In such moments, we cry out as Job did. In God's absence, we cry out for help and healing.

As you are able and willing, write about these times in your life.

_____

_____

_____

_____

_____

_____

_____

CHAPTER 6: SPIRIT

_____
_____
_____
_____
_____
_____
_____
_____
_____
_____
_____
_____
_____
_____
_____
_____
_____
_____
_____
_____
_____
_____
_____
_____
_____
_____
_____
_____
_____
_____

DAY 7

BETTER TOGETHER

Read Genesis 2:4–25

Then the LORD God said, "It is not good that the man should be alone." (v. 18)

WE READ THIS PASSAGE EARLIER and focused on the creation of Adam. Today we will think about the creation of Eve. In his book *Storyline: Finding Your Subplot in God's Story*, Donald Miller writes beautifully about the creation of Eve. He notes that initially it was just Adam who walked the earth. During this time Adam was in contact with his Maker. He watched God fashion the many creatures of the earth and even gave them names. In many ways it must have been a wonderful time.

But still something was missing. Though the animals were delightful and kept Adam company, there was no creature like Adam, no creation for him to share his life with. Even with the company of God and all the creatures, Adam was lonely. God recognized this need and fashioned one like Adam, made from his own rib. When Adam saw the one so like himself but yet different, he cried out with joy, "Bone of my bone and flesh of my flesh" (v. 23).

As social creatures we have a need to be with those who are like unto us. When our family suffered the loss of a beloved family dog, no member of our family missed him more than our other pup. We tried to comfort and console our surviving dog in his grief. We petted him, played with him, and took him on outings he would enjoy. But still, something was missing.

As days turned into weeks, our dog continued to mope about the house. He was glad for our presence, but we were not enough.

He formed a habit of licking and biting his tail to the point of bleeding. After a vet suggested Xanax as a treatment for our mourning dog, we decided to take action.

One Saturday we took our dog out to visit a dachshund we had seen advertised in the paper. This perky new pooch immediately took to our family, and slowly our sad pup began to change. We found him playing with and then cuddling with the new dog. He found joy in walks and car rides again when he had a buddy along. A couple of weeks later, as I was petting both dogs, I sneaked a peek at our first dog's tail. I could not believe what I saw! What had been a raw, bloody wound had healed and was almost entirely covered with new fur.

Like our hound, we were not meant to be alone. It is not good for our health and well-being. Isolation can result in self-destructive behaviors, but great joy is found with companionship.

Daily Exercise: Group Singing

Singing in and of itself is a very therapeutic exercise. It combines the benefits of breathing with the lift of music on the soul. When we join our voice with the voices of others in group singing, it seems the benefits to our social and mental health are multiplied, an idea that recent research supports.[14] Any longtime choir member or frequent concert attendee will tell you that the exercise of singing together is bonding and uplifting in a way that is hard to explain.

Today we will look for an opportunity for group singing. Maybe you can attend a church where hymns or choruses are sung. Maybe you can plan to attend a concert with friends or a sporting event where the national anthem will be sung. If there is no other opportunity, you can go for a drive with a buddy, turn up the radio, and sing along! As you sing, note the feel of your voice, the vibrations in your throat. Get a full inhalation and let the words and sound flow out of you. We are called to make a joyful noise . . . though some of us are a bit noisier than others!

Reflection

What was your experience of singing with someone or with a group? Having sung in several choirs, I can attest to what it feels like to put in time, effort, and practice, and then have the experience of lifting that song with others. Community is important—not just being around people but participating in activities together. There are groups that gather to knit and write, to ride bicycles and run, to work and help.

Today, write a bit about how you have participated in one of these groups, either by singing with others today or in your past. Think of an activity you did with others where you felt joined together.

_____

_____

_____

_____

_____

_____

_____

_____

_____

_____

_____

_____

_____

_____

_____

_____

_____

_____

_____

_____

CHAPTER 6 REVIEW

This week involved struggling with how we relate to God in the midst of our anxiety. How have you previously reconciled (or struggled to reconcile) your anxiety with your spirituality?

Perhaps there were words of judgment that you used against yourself (or others) who experience anxiety. Write down those words, not as a way of agreeing with them, but to acknowledge them.

Now consider words of grace that you may have read or felt from God this week regarding your anxiety. Take some time to note these as well.

Which Scripture passages or exercises brought you a greater sense of peace about dealing with anxiety as a Christian?

Are there places that you still struggle with dealing with anxiety as a Christian?

We can still struggle with our need for control, often expressed in rules and laws and how well (or poorly) we follow them, but ultimately this is God's work, not ours. This week has been one to explore God's grace and love and acceptance for you . . . even in the places where you may feel hurt or even broken. God has not given up on you—never has and never will. In the midst of the waves, the hand of Jesus is reaching out again.

CHAPTER 7

COMMUNITY

DAY 1

GOING BACK TO COMMUNITY

Read 1 Kings 19:11–18

Then the LORD said to him, "Go, return on your way to the wilderness of Damascus." (v. 15)

THIS IS THE THIRD TIME we have read from 1 Kings 19. First, we read of Elijah's flight after Jezebel made threats against his life. Then we reflected on Elijah's exhaustion under the broom tree. Now we follow as Elijah travels to Mount Horeb, the mountain of God, to wait for God to pass by. In this beautiful passage, we read how God came to Elijah, but not in the wind or the earthquake or even the fire. Instead, God is found in the silence. After encountering the whisper of God in this silence, Elijah speaks his worries and hurt. He tells God how zealous he had been and how unfaithful the rest of the Israelites were. He exclaims, "I *alone* am left, and they are seeking my life, to take it away" (v. 14, emphasis mine).

I especially feel for Elijah in this moment. We have all had times when we feel isolated from our communities. We feel frustrated and betrayed by their actions. We no longer feel connected with them. Moreover, we no longer feel safe. We go off by ourselves, feeling utterly alone. God hears Elijah's pleas against the community of Israelites. The surprising part is how God responds. *God tells Elijah to go back.* God names the people that will be of help to Elijah. Furthermore, he informs Elijah that he is not the only one who has remained faithful in the turmoil: there are seven thousand others who have not bowed to the foreign god Baal.

It is very hard when our communities disappoint us. Unfortunately, sooner or later it will happen to all of us. Communities are made of people, and people are imperfect. But after we have traveled away and poured out our sadness, frustration, and anger to God, after God ministers to us through angels, bread, and silence, it is time to go back. We must take a deep breath, gather our courage, and give people another try. Though it may seem we are all alone, there are always people who can be of help to us that we have simply not met yet. There are always others out there like us; we have just lost sight of them in our weariness and fear.

When Elijah leaves the mountain to return to the wilderness, he meets Elisha—Elisha, who will become his devoted disciple. We too will meet new faces, people who will turn into close friends. But first, we will take a moment to pause in that sheer silence, to watch for God to pass by. There we will breathe and be renewed so we are ready to engage community again.

Daily Exercise: Centering Prayer

Today we will learn the ancient spiritual practice of centering prayer. This practice is very similar to mindfulness meditation. One main difference is that, instead of following the breath, centering prayer uses a centering word to anchor us into God's presence. Before you begin, pick the centering word you will repeat throughout this practice. It is best if this is a fairly neutral word that does not bring up strong emotions or reactions. If you cannot think of a word, you can simply use "God" or "thou." As we did with mindfulness meditation, you may want to set a timer for ten minutes.

Find a comfortable, quiet, seated position, and take a few deep breaths. Start by repeating the centering word to yourself as a way to bring yourself into an awareness of God's presence. Each time a thought comes to mind, use the centering word to draw yourself back to resting in the presence of God. Eventually, you will get carried away by a particular thought trail. When you realize this has happened, simply release the thought and use your centering word to bring you back to resting with God. No judgment or frustration is necessary. You are not failing or doing badly. We all get distracted by our many thoughts. Simply practice coming back again and again to a restfulness in God's presence using the anchor of the centering word. If you get too tired or frustrated, let the practice go for now. Again, you have not failed. You have practiced, and that is what matters. If you are still centering yourself with the word when the timer goes off, release the word. Gradually take some deep breaths and come back to an awareness of your physical surroundings. Slowly stretch as you open your eyes. Take note of how your body, mind, and spirit feel at the end of this practice. Know that you can return to it whenever you wish.

Reflection

Communities can hurt us as well as heal us. Many of us have experienced communities that were nurturing and healing. We trust our communities because of that healing. But this is why our communities also have the ability to hurt us so deeply. We assumed the community was safe. We assumed that no matter what past hurts we brought with us, the community would accept us. But communities, even church communities, are made of broken people.

When a community hurts us, it is difficult not to let that hurt define us or affect our willingness to experience community. Eventually, when the hurt has lessened, we can reenter community (the same one or perhaps a different one), knowing that one experience is not all of our experience. Just because a few people were hurtful does not mean all people will be.

Jesus frequently called people who were "broken" or excluded from the community back into the community. This included people who had injuries, diseases, and were disabled, people with jobs that others did not like (like tax collectors), or people who had been mistreated. Jesus did not allow the opinions of others to change how he saw people. And the same is true for you.

Take a few moments and consider what opinions you have

received from your communities. How have these stopped you from being a part of the group? What would happen if you treated these opinions like those "thought trails" in the centering prayer exercise and went back to that community anyway?

DAY 2

RESPECTING OUR LIMITS

Read Proverbs 27:17

Iron sharpens iron, and one person sharpens the wits of another.

THE GIFT OF RELATIONSHIP IS a recurring theme in the Bible. In Proverbs 27, a chapter filled with advice on relationships, we are reminded that we are to each other as *iron sharpening iron.* This verse reminds me of many friends who have made me a better person by simply being in my life. Even as I remember their gift to me, I know I have encouraged them as well, because iron sharpening iron is a mutual process. If only one blade rubs across the other, the iron will be sharpened in a lopsided way. Only one side of the blade will be sharp and the other side will remain dull. For best results, the blades need to take turns sharpening each other so there is an even sharpness of both sides, and the blades will be in peak form.

A partner exercise I teach in yoga class also reminds me of the truth of Proverbs 27:17. In this exercise two people sit back-to-back. We breathe together for a minute, just soaking in the awareness that someone has "got our back," literally feeling each other's support. Then we take turns doing two poses. One person folds forward as if they will touch their toes. Then the second person leans back against them, coming into a backbend position. It is a brilliant setup as the forward-folding position is getting a deeper stretch from the backbender's weight. At the same time, the backbender is getting a wonderful moment of support, opening, and release. But then we switch poses. The backbender becomes the forward folder, now taking on the role of the one who is challenged. Similarly, the forward folder now becomes the backbender, taking their turn to rest against their partner for support and release.

This sequence is a lovely bonding moment between friends, but the best part is that we always switch sides. If one person always gave the support, they would eventually be overstretched and injured; our bodies have limits. Our physical forms can only give so much, stretch so much, support so much weight. If we push ourselves past these limits, damage occurs. Moreover, if the one receiving support never takes a turn at being challenged, their body would become unbalanced. If the backbender stayed in the pose indefinitely, their chest and shoulders would eventually become too open and their legs would get weak and stiff, unable to hold their own weight.

The point is this: relationships were made to be expressions of mutuality. People who struggle with anxiety tend to be givers, caretakers, or people pleasers. After years of helping others, anyone can become worn, tired, and, in many ways, injured. Healthy communities for us will be ones of mutuality, where we are not only challenged and stretched but also supported. Our limits must always be respected by ourselves and others, and we should respect the needs of others to strengthen themselves by letting us lean on them for a while.

If this environment of mutuality is not the case for you, just take note of that. Sometimes there is hope of change in a lopsided relationship. If we recognize our pattern of overgiving, we may be able to seek balance in our relationships again. Our partners, given the chance, may come around to this idea as well. But there are times where relationships become so unbalanced and hurtful that the healthiest thing we can do is walk away. But we are not there yet (more on healthy boundaries coming on day 5). For now we observe, notice, and bring awareness to the patterns of giving and receiving.

Daily Exercise: Yoga Partner Exercise
Ask a friend or someone you trust if they would like to enjoy this partner yoga series with you. It may be wise to avoid choosing

someone with whom you are currently having conflict. Try to let this be a playful moment for the both of you. This is not some test of your relationship or a moment of confrontation. Just let it be an experience you both can play with and enjoy.

First, sit back-to-back on the floor and breathe while sensing each other's presence at your backs. Then let the person wearing a lighter colored shirt fold forward as far as is comfortable for them. Set a timer for three minutes. Now the person wearing a darker colored shirt will slowly lean back on their forward-folding partner. As you do this keep asking them, "Is this okay? How do you feel? More or less pressure?" If they do not feel comfortable holding your whole weight, use your arms to support yourself while still resting partially on their back. Try to relax into your respective poses and breaths. When the timer sounds, the backbender will sit up and the forward folder will follow.

Now switch poses with the person wearing the darker colored shirt folding forward as far as is comfortable as the other partner sets the timer for three minutes. Then the backbender will lean back slowly, supporting themselves a bit with their arms. Remember to ask for feedback. "Is this okay? Do you want me to lean back more or less?" When you get to a comfortable place together, breathe for the remainder of the three minutes. When the timer sounds, the backbender rises up first and then the forward folder.

The success of this exercise does not come from how deeply one person was able to fold or how completely they held your weight, but from the practice of taking turns and playing together with this partner exercise. Finish by coming again to an upright, back-to-back position. Enjoy the sensation of "having each other's backs." Finally, thank each other for sharing in this practice together.

Reflection

In week 5, you drew a map that asked you to look at the relationships in your life. Which relationships are draining and which are life giving and supporting? Today (and tomorrow), we look again at this aspect of your life.

This is not a call to systematically discard people who are "problems" in your life. The more challenging but ultimately more fulfilling route can be to have an honest conversation. After all, there may be a misunderstanding of the relationship, a problem in what they expect and what you expect from them. Deeper relationship is built on sharing the good and the difficult, and committing to growing through all of it together.

So consider the relationships in your life. Perhaps there is someone with whom you need to have that honest conversation. Perhaps use the space below to practice that conversation. You may also consider someone you feel you have relied on too much. How would you have an equally honest conversation with them to restore the balance?

_____

_____

_____

_____

_____

_____

_____

_____

_____

_____

_____

_____

_____

_____

_____

_____

_____

_____

DAY 3

COMMUNITIES IN FLUX

Read Acts 10:44–48

"Can anyone withhold the water for baptizing these people who have received the Holy Spirit just as we have?"
(v. 47)

PETER HAS BEEN SUMMONED BY divine circumstances to the home of Cornelius, a centurion and more importantly a Gentile who lives in Caesarea. Peter has been asked to share his story with them. As Peter is telling Cornelius and his company about Jesus, something amazing happens. The Holy Spirit falls upon the hearers just as he fell upon those assembled at Pentecost.

Peter and his companions were astounded, not imagining this scenario was possible. Before this time the followers of Jesus had mainly been comprised of a group of twelve Jewish men. The group of followers had expanded among a group of Galilean Jews, but this was still a pretty small, very similar group.

Now we have the gospel of Jesus moving out of Israel and the Jewish nation to non-Jewish members of the Roman army. Are Peter and the disciples going to hold on to this same community they have known for these past few years, or are they going to allow their community to flex and grow to receive these new faces?

Human nature makes it tempting to cling to what we know. If we have a group we trust and rely on, then we probably want to keep these people in our lives for as long as possible. But life is no respecter of our holding on. Friends move. Loved ones die. Churches change. The only thing we can depend on is that our community will not stay the same forever.

But change can be good as well! God can bring new people

into our lives, even though we wonder if we can open up and trust them as much as our old friends.

As Peter and his group wonder this about the new Gentile faces, something happens that helps them allow their community to change: the Holy Spirit moves. Since the anointing of the Holy Spirit upon these unexpected candidates is so clear and similar to their own anointing, Peter and the other followers see the only correct choice is to baptize these new friends. With this act the bounds of their community move, widen, and flex in beautiful and challenging ways.

We will not always see such a clear movement of the Holy Spirit, but we can become sensitive to the ways the Spirit is calling us to allow movement and fluidity in our communities. Change is never easy, especially when it concerns our relationships, but hopefully we can listen and look for how the Spirit is flowing and moving in our communal life.

Daily Exercise: Coloring Your Relationship Circles

Today we are going to engage in an exercise from a book by Sybil MacBeth called *Praying in Color*. We have modified the exercise somewhat to fit our present purpose.

As you did in week 5, think again about the relationships in your life. Make a time (perhaps fifteen minutes) when you have some quiet and privacy. Gather some paper and colored pencils or markers. Start by drawing out the primary communities in your life (e.g., immediate family, family of origin, church groups, book club, friends, neighbors, and others). Draw big circles (or whatever shape you wish) for the most important communities in your life and smaller circles for those that are in your life but not as prominent. If you have lots of colors, you can make each community a different shade.

Take some time to reflect on your relationship with each of these communities. Are you feeling refreshed by your connection to each particular group? Is there a group that frustrates you because it either constantly drains your energy or no longer seems to give you any support?

After you have considered the groups that are already present in your life, ponder if there are any new groups or communities that may be calling to you. Is there a person you are feeling the urge to get to know a little more?

Using new colors, redraw your circles. Draw larger circles around the communities you already have in which you would like to deepen your connection. Draw new circles for the people and groups you would like to bring into your life. Feel free to draw as many circles as you wish. Let them make a beautiful pattern on your page. Have an open heart for how God might use them to bless you (and how you might bless them).

Inside the circles of those communities that seem to be going stale or bringing only frustration to your life, draw smaller circles. As you do this, feel grace in that choice. Lessening the presence of a community in your life does not have to include anger or judgment (although with primary relationships such as close friends this can be challenging). Sometimes we just are not able to give to others in the same way we once were, and sometimes others are not able to give to us as much as we would like them to. As much as possible let there be a flow of love and forgiveness even as you make the choice to diminish contact with these people in your life. In most cases, you will not remove these people's presence in your life; you will merely lessen their prominence.

Look back over your collection of circles. Know that even this collection of colors and shape sizes is not permanent. Our communities often move and adjust throughout our life, much like the pieces of a kaleidoscope move into different patterns. Just because some pieces move away and others take their place to form a new pattern, they all are beautiful in their own way. In fact, if you want to draw some overarching pattern or make lines that connect these communities to represent the Spirit's flow in your life, do that as well. As you move your pencil around the representations of the people in your life, say a prayer for all of them and your connection to each of them. Ask God to continue to bless your relationships even as you hold them with open hands.

Reflection

Day 3 is typically about movement, stretching, and that is what you were asked to do in today's daily exercise. You were not asked to make a decision but to simply look for where some relationships may need some stretching and maybe where you need to be stretched as well.

God loves us too much to allow us to remain the same. Although the journey of faith often feels like turmoil and trial, such times stretch us. Without that stretching, there is not room for growth.

Where are you being asked to move and grow? Where do you think God is stretching you? Finally, what relationships are you being asked to stretch with and through?

_____

_____

_____

_____

_____

_____

_____

_____

_____

_____

_____

_____

_____

_____

_____

_____

_____

DAY 4

BEING OF ONE MIND

Read Ecclesiastes 4:9–12

And though one might prevail against another, two will withstand one. A threefold cord is not quickly broken. (v. 12)

WHEN I FIRST BEGAN SWIMMING laps as an adult, I shared a pool lane with Jason and trailed behind him as he swam. I learned that if I swam in the current he created, it would pull me along. This act of trailing a more advanced swimmer helped me go faster and longer than I could on my own. In stark contrast to this, sometimes our water aerobics instructor would have our class swim in a circle around the pool. All would go well until the moment she would call out for us to switch directions. Then there was a large group of people, in a large circle, in a large pool, all moving against the current we had created. Not only would I lose any forward momentum I had built up, sometimes I would even find myself moving backward in the powerful current, no matter how hard I swam against it.

These same principles can apply to our communal life. When we look at the groups we spend time with, it is wise to discern how they may or may not support the healing truths we are incorporating as a part of our anxiety management. There will surely be times when the negative thoughts we struggle with will rear up and threaten to wreak havoc upon us. It will be in these moments that the people who surround us can make a big difference, that they can "lift up the other" (v. 10). If we have friends and family who share the truths we have claimed in our healing, they will become for us like the strands of the cord to which the writer of

Ecclesiastes refers. Even when our own mind begins to fray with the wear of our negative thoughts, our friends will come beside us and hold us, strengthening us and keeping us from breaking under the power of our hurtful thoughts.

However, if we continue to be around people and groups that play into our negative thoughts, our healing may be hindered. Most people who struggle with anxiety or depression find it a challenge to see the strength God has given us, to believe we are a beloved child of God. We are not typically the ones who need someone to urge us to think less of ourselves or about ourselves.

Remember that Jesus spoke different truths to the Pharisees (or religious leaders) than he spoke to those who were hurt and broken. Both messages were about a God who loves all of us and wants a relationship with all of us. To the religious leaders, he kept saying to get out of the way. Those who were hurt and felt broken he invited in. The more you are with people who know well the truths you are still learning, the more they will pull you along on the journey to wholeness and joy.

Remember the pool at the beginning of this chapter. The people in your life will create a current one way or the other. Just make sure the current is headed in the direction God is calling you with people who support you and can be strength for you.

Daily Exercise: Writing a Creed

Many churches have a creed or statement of faith, usually a written statement or verbal acknowledgment of what they hold to be true about their faith. Many of these begin with a statement like "I believe in God, the Almighty, maker of heaven and earth . . ."

Consider taking some time today to write your own creed. This creed will not necessarily be a statement about your faith in general, such as what you believe about God. Instead, think about what you are learning to be true about God for you and the relationships in your life and the nature of your journey. Dena's creed would begin by claiming her status as a beloved child of God and acknowledging she believes all people are worthy of love and care. She would then go on to talk about her God-given need for rest and creativity, as well as her need to participate in meaningful work.

Your creed may sound different. Whatever shape your statement takes, let it be a reflection of what you are coming to understand as true in your own life. Let it reflect the values and actions that are vital for you.

After you have written your creed, let it be a guide for what kind of "currents" you need to be looking for. Are your present communities flowing in this general direction? Are there some groups around you that you could join that would pull you further along in the flow?

Reflection

It is important to recognize the difference between *belief* and *faith*. In our context here, belief is more of a statement, a list of propositions, a set of facts. While these are most certainly important, they are not the same as faith. Faith is more about journeying with God. It is a relationship of reliance and trust, even when the path that you are walking is difficult. It is a relationship where we know God is with us in the midst of the wind and the waves. We may still be afraid, but we trust that in the end, all will be well.

The very tricky part for those of us with anxiety is that beliefs can often be a way we exercise control. It may be the way we feel in control because of how we understand or believe. We may even say to ourselves, "As long as I believe this, that, and the other, then everything is fine."

But we are not in control. God is. And God will not be bound, even by our beliefs about God!

Consider writing about how your beliefs are different from your relationship with God. Think about which of your beliefs may need to flex as you live in relationship with God.

DAY 5

HAVING HEALTHY BOUNDARIES

Read 2 Corinthians 9:7-9

*Each of you must give as you have made up your mind,
not reluctantly or under compulsion, for God loves a
cheerful giver. (v. 7)*

OUR CLERGYMAN RECITES THIS VERSE every Sunday at the offering time. I admit, at first I thought it was a nudge to persuade people to give more money. In my life I have often heard the last part of this verse recited manipulatively. Whether in preparation for a building campaign or Sunday school teacher recruitment, the verse "God loves a cheerful giver" was used as code language for "Cough up your time and money now, and be happy about it!"

However, as I listened to this whole verse week after week in church, I actually began *reducing* both the time and money I was giving each Sunday. This was not some passive-aggressive move on my part in response to being asked. Rather, it was a response that came out of a new understanding of the passage. God does not want me to give of myself and my resources to the point of exhaustion and anger. God wants me to give from my abundance and joy. If I am grumbling every time I write a check or teach a Sunday school class, then maybe it is time to back off for a while and fill back up until I can give cheerfully again.

I think this verse is useful for more than just our church life. Our friends, our family, and our work all place demands on us that, left unchecked, will lead to bitterness and exhaustion. It is up to us to take off the fake smile, look at what we actually have within us to give, and learn to better manage our offering to others. In contemporary language, we need to develop some boundaries. Our time, our energy, and our riches are all in limited supply. We have to learn to say yes when we can do so willingly and honestly. And we also have to learn to say no firmly when we are at the end of our resources.

When we have strong boundaries in place to protect ourselves physically, emotionally, and spiritually, our anxiety is more likely to be kept at bay. We are then able to make self-care a regular priority. We will be able to limit our exposure to stress. And we will be able to make the choice to leave an anxiety-producing situation when needed so we do not end up in a flared-up state from which it is difficult to recover.

Developing healthy boundaries takes practice, but over time we can find ourselves giving, not with sighs of regret but with sounds of joy.

Daily Exercise: Practice Setting a Boundary

Look for a moment in your day when you are asked to do something you really do not wish to do. Start small. Maybe a family member asks you to run an errand or babysit for them. Maybe a coworker asks you to help them with a project that is not your responsibility. All these requests play into a negative thought pattern that anxiety sufferers often share: *I am the only one who can take care of this. In the end, it is all up to me. No one else will do this like it needs to be done.*

These thoughts are not true. There are often others who can handle problems instead of you. Not every problem has to be solved anyway, and certainly not by you. When you encounter a problem that is not life threatening, not your responsibility, or simply not something you wish to do during the course of this day, try something.

Try saying, "No."

If you are new to saying no, a short, simple version is often best. You do not have to apologize or justify yourself. You may just say, "No, I can't do that," or, "I am unable to do that today," or, "I'm sorry, I'm already committed to something else." And you are. You are committed to your own well-being. Notice how you feel as you say no and set your boundary. You can observe how it was received, but do not get too caught up in the reactions of others. You are not responsible for their emotions and reactions, only your own. Notice how you feel later on in the day after setting your boundary. If this is an unsettling experience for you, be gracious with this feeling. Over time you will get more and more confident in setting a firm boundary and finding your strong no.

Reflection

Today you were asked to say no. Today is also the day of the week in which we have been practicing change. Since saying no takes practice and perhaps some useful phrases, think of some creative ways to say no that would work for you. These could range from "Let me check my calendar and get back with you" to a more honest "I just don't think I can say yes right now and mean it." Write down some possible statements you could use to set your boundary.

_____

_____

_____

_____

_____

_____

_____

_____

_____

_____

_____

_____

DAY 6

AUTHENTICITY IN COMMUNITY

Read 2 Corinthians 4:5–10

But we have this treasure in clay jars, so that it may be made clear that this extraordinary power belongs to God and does not come from us. (v. 7)

WE HAVE ALL BEEN IN situations where we did not feel we could be ourselves. Certain groups and situations make us feel like we need to put on a mask of perfection—or at least a shinier, more made-up version of ourselves—to be acceptable. This may be okay for the occasional cocktail party or meeting, but it is cause for concern when our core communities and faith gatherings are places where authenticity is not possible.

There is a worrisome trend in Christianity of sending the message that being a Christian means you are no longer sinful or imperfect. Of course, we are all hoping to be made more perfect by the power of the Holy Spirit, but let's be honest: we are all more than a little imperfect a lot of the time. We are all still human, and we are all still sinners. We are flawed and limited beings.

The hard thing about anxiety is that most of the time our worry and struggles are about things others cannot see. If we were to be injured in a car wreck or battling cancer, those struggles would be visible to those around us. We would likely share them with those around us and then receive support. However, anxiety can be so invisible. Others cannot see the hardship and damage it causes us. The invisibility of anxiety is often compounded by its stigma. Whether there is actual judgment or only fear of judgment about our worries and weaknesses, we often do not feel safe sharing our invisible struggles with our faith community—a place we would ideally receive help and support.

The good news is many faith communities are reclaiming the value of honesty and authenticity that Paul knew to be so vital in a faith journey. We are not perfect. But God is. Somehow if we risk being honest about our struggles and show our authentic selves, God will not receive less glory but more. For even we, flawed beings that we are, are miraculously able to make a difference in this world. We can love and comfort and grow beauty in the midst of our imperfection. And all this happens by the power of God working through us, for ours is not a God of condemnation and judgment, but a God of grace and healing and salvation in the midst of our difficulties.

The wonderful thing about being a lamp made of clay is our cracks and nicks only make us more usable. It is the thinnest places in a clay lamp, not the strongest places, that let the light shine through.

The first church where I served had beautiful stained glass windows. If the original sheets of glass had remained intact and perfect, they would have been quite lovely. But when they were broken, the artist was able to combine them into images and patterns that were much more meaningful and beautiful than just sheets of colored glass.

I hope you are able to find communities and specifically a faith community that allows you to be honest and authentic about your brokenness, remembering that God's Spirit moves in and through those broken and open spaces. Such a community is an oasis of grace, a true gift as you learn to break past the fear of stigma and make your invisible struggles known. Once we own our weakness as clay vessels, we are able to receive much-needed support from others and we are able to serve our Savior in ways we could not have imagined. The power of our healing is a grace that comes from above. Thanks be to God!

Daily Exercise: Requesting Support or Prayer

Often with anxiety we struggle with things about which we would never breathe a word to others. The stifling of our worries and concerns only makes them grow stronger.

Today, think of a group of people with whom you could begin to risk being honest. Maybe you participate in a small group or book club. Maybe it is the group with whom you are going through this study! Think of times when this group presents opportunities for you to share your concerns.

If your group takes prayer concerns or participates in prayers of the people, this could be a great opportunity to name your need for prayer and support. Asking someone else to support you, and especially to pray for you, takes vulnerability. But it is a huge step toward living honestly and authentically with a group of people.

Reflection

It is a deep spiritual truth for us as Christians that in our broken-ness, we are made whole. Somehow in the "emptying out" of Jesus on the cross salvation comes. Paul writes so eloquently that this is "foolishness" to those who consider themselves wise and learned (1 Cor. 1:23). We are a people who experience our own Good Fridays, but we know that Easter and resurrection are on the way.

Take a few moments to think of your own moments of vulnerability that ended in a wonderful surprise. Consider a time when you risked being open and honest and received a deeper, more authentic relationship in return. Consider the places in your life where being vulnerable and open may be healing for you and others.

_____

_____

_____

_____

_____

_____

DAY 7

PASSING IT FORWARD

Read Deuteronomy 24:17–22

Remember that you were a slave in the land of Egypt;
therefore I am commanding you to do this. (v. 22)

In this passage from Deuteronomy, the Israelites are instructed to care for those in need. When they encounter immigrants, widows, and orphans they are asked to share some of their resources with those who are in a vulnerable place. This passage and indeed the whole of Deuteronomy is punctuated with the message that the Israelites should do this with the knowledge of their own poverty and vulnerability when they were slaves in Egypt.

One of the silver linings of hardship is that once we have survived it we become more compassionate to others who are suffering. We know what difficult times feel like. Having this knowledge, we are not only sensitive to the needs of others but capable of reaching out to them in a way that others may not be.

You may have experienced this already. There may be others who have gone before you in the struggle with anxiety and have helped you along your path. There may be other friends in your life who struggle with anxiety or similar issues now. You may have already reached out to them so the two of you can walk together. If you have not already shared your story and words of advice with someone more overwhelmed than you, that day will likely come.

As you ponder the mystery of the great cloud of witnesses (Heb. 12:1) that cheers each of us along in life, know that you are not only one of the runners but one who cheers others on as well. Let us think through this call to reach out and give a hand to our sisters and brothers who struggle!

If you are still in a place where you are struggling in anxiety's grip, be careful how many of your resources you let yourself give away. While it is true that two are often better than one, it can also be the case that a friend who is drowning under the waves of fear and chaos will unintentionally reach out and pull you under in their attempts to stay afloat. You want to be careful to protect your boundaries, giving from the abundance of your resources and not to your own detriment. Know that there will be times when you can help a struggling friend and other times when you have to walk away to maintain your own health. There is no guilt in this. To be good for others, you must have some strength left.

But as you are able, look for ways to be generous to others struggling with anxiety. Today's exercise will help you think through how you might do this.

Daily Exercise: Looking Ahead

Today you are going to think ahead in your story and imagine a time when you have been set free from your enslavement to fear. You are going to imagine a time beyond your period of wandering through the wild paths of healing and recovery. You are going to imagine yourself in a land where you are maintaining your health and well-being.

Picture the day in this place when a friend or an acquaintance comes to you and shares a bit of their story. What they say rings true with you because they are in the midst of a struggle with anxiety.

When this happens, you want to be empowered not only to lend a listening ear but to give aid to your struggling friend. What will you say? How will you share your own story so that their walls of stigma and isolation come down? How will you let them know they are not alone? What resources will you share with them?

What techniques and changes in your life have made enough of a difference that you want to pass them along to another? Are there any words of encouragement you can give them? Any paths of healing you want to point them toward? Is there anything else you would want to say or do to give grace to this one in need?

Take a few moments to imagine this conversation.

After you have finished reflecting on this exchange, give thanks for the grace of healing, both your own and for the healing of others that you will play a part in.

Reflection

In Deuteronomy 5, we have the second version of the Ten Commandments. The first version is in Exodus 20. The main difference in these two is the framing of the commandment to observe the Sabbath. The version in Deuteronomy 5 says, "Remember that you were slaves in Egypt" (v. 15 NIV). This is not a far cry from "Do to others as you would have them do to you" (Luke 6:31).

One of the foundations of our faith is empathy. We read many times about how God felt for the people and acted. We are called to feel for one another and act on this feeling too! Our communities are places where we should receive support and care, but also places where we should be supportive and caring.

Think of a time when you have been helpful to someone else, when you have contributed to your community. It does not have to be about anxiety management. It could be any time when you have helped with a word or project, with listening or a helping hand. Write about that time.

_____

_____

_____

_____

_____

_____

CHAPTER 7: COMMUNITY

CHAPTER 7 REVIEW

How have communities helped you in your struggle with anxiety?

When have communities hurt you in your journey with anxiety?

What are the relationships that nurture you and help you be your best self?

Are there places you need to set clearer boundaries or pull back from unhealthy relationships?

How is your current church community helpful or unhelpful to you as you learn to manage your anxiety?

Who are the people you can share your story with?

Human relationships contain a sort of tension, a push and pull, and a commitment to being on a journey together. In many ways this reflects our journey with God in that there are times of intense closeness and times we feel distant. But our relationships with other people are different from our relationship with God, as there are occasions when we may need to choose better boundaries and healthier, more supportive relationships. In moving through this chapter, we pray you have gained some clarity on communities that support your own journey with anxiety.

CHAPTER 8

COMMISSIONING

We have experienced seven weeks of seven days together. Hopefully through the course of these seven weeks, you have learned some new skills. You have tried something new that surprised you. Your awareness of and ability to manage your anxiety has improved.

But this is a book about our faith as well as anxiety. There is a next step. It is the eighth day.

Let us explain.

In early Christian communities there was a strong awareness that what had happened on Easter was a radical re-creation of the world. Many of the earliest followers of Christ continued to worship in the synagogue and temple, observing the Sabbath, or what would be Saturday for us. But they also worshipped on Sunday. This was the first day of the week or day 1. There are early Christian writings that refer to this as being the "eighth day," placing an emphasis on the new thing that was happening, a day that was about newness and re-creation.

We think an eighth week is an important reminder that you are living as a new being, a new creation of yourself. As you go through this week, consider the ways you have already been living in a new way. Consider where you have felt different and new. Look for the places where there is new life springing forth for you.

Another important aspect of this week, and why we have titled it "Commissioning," is that it is a week of going forth. The disciples were told to "go and tell," and where we have felt healing or help, that is our task too.

COMING BACK TO THE BREATH

Read Genesis 1

In the beginning when God created the heavens and the earth, the earth was a formless void and darkness covered the face of the deep, while a wind from God swept over the face of the waters. (vv. 1–2)

TODAY WE REVISIT ONE OF the first passages we read together in this book. In doing so, we remember not only the beginning of the world but also the beginning of our time together in this journey of healing. As we look back on this first day of chapter 8, we remember that it all started with the breath.

As we read in Genesis, the beginning was darkness and chaos. Then God brought order and life and creativity to the formless void. In that moment, God breathed. After a deep inhalation, God's exhalation sent a wind over the face of the deep. After having breathed, God spoke light and order and life into the world. That big breath set the stage for God's intense work of creating heaven and earth from the formless void.

When we feel the waters of chaos rising and the darkness closing in, let us take God's lead and go back to our breath. When the deep darkness swirls around and within, remember to use the breath as a reset button to take you back to the beginning. When we can take a moment or two (or ten) to inhale and exhale deeply, we can remember how to tame the chaotic waters around us instead of just being fearful of their threat. Because anxiety is very good at spinning out terrifying what-if scenarios, a focus on just one breath at a time helps ground us in the present instead of spiraling us through future possibilities.

We can only breathe for *right now*, for this present moment.

As you go into the rest of your journey with anxiety management, know that the closest resource will always be your breath. If you can remember how to tune into the breath's flow, if you can remember how to deepen and slow its pace, then you will always have a way to calm your body and mind in any circumstance.

Through this book, we have given you several breathing practices to play with, but now it is time for you to identify and claim those that are the easiest and most helpful for you. We hope these forms of breathwork will become an everyday part of your life. Practicing is important so that eventually the exercise becomes second nature for you. When fear rises and your body tenses, may your mind and body's automatic response be to breathe. May this breath be an anchor for you in any and all storms that come your way.

Daily Exercise: Breath Exercise of Your Choice

Many churches follow a cycle of readings during the year, and while part of us might say, "Yes, I've heard that before," hearing a familiar passage again often brings new insights and meaning. Perhaps even as you read this passage from Genesis there was some new word for you. Revisiting is important, but recognize that each time you revisit, you have changed and therefore may interact with a passage, a place, or a practice in a different way.

As we return to the "beginning," think back to a breathing exercise that was particularly helpful or appealing to you. Was it belly breath, breath prayer, counted breath, or some other technique? Today practice your favorite breathing exercise from the past seven weeks. Consider how it may have felt awkward and unfamiliar, but now it feels like home.

As you make time and space for that breathing exercise now, know that you can continue to weave this practice into your daily life. Is there a time of day when you can dedicate five or ten minutes to a breath exercise? Can you start the morning with a breath prayer? Can you end the day with counted breath? Can you do five minutes of belly breathing at lunchtime to calm and refocus you midday?

Even as your practice of breathing has begun to feel like home over these weeks, know that feeling will deepen as you continue these practices over the course of your life. No matter what situation or circumstance you may find yourself in, the breath will always be there for you, has always been there for you.

Reflection

We have heard it said many times that long journeys begin with just one step. But often before you take that first step into something new or challenging, before you start . . . you stop. You breathe. Then you step forward.

On this first day of this eighth week, consider the journey ahead. Know that it will have some twists and turns because all journeys do. While this day is framed as a restarting, a re-creation, we begin each day in the same way: with a single step. Consider what actions you take that are "first steps" or "beginnings." Maybe it is the breath or that pause you take in bed before climbing out. Maybe it is the last moment that you sit in the car before going inside. Maybe it is that first step of a long walk.

Today write a bit about "beginnings" that led you forward, focusing on these steps and not the whole journey. Avoid focusing on "missteps," even though those can be important to your journey too! Instead, think graciously about beginnings that have been like that first breath, that have shone light on your path, that have filled your world with color and sound and living things.

_____

_____

_____

_____

_____

_____

DAY 2

THE BODY YOU TAKE WITH YOU

Read John 20:24–29

Then he said to Thomas, "Put your finger here and see my hands. Reach out your hand and put it in my side. Do not doubt but believe." (v. 27)

AS WE READ IN AN earlier chapter, Jesus appears to the disciples following his death and resurrection, telling them "Peace be with you" (v. 26) and breathing the Holy Spirit upon them. What an amazing event these disciples shared.

But Thomas was not there. When he did arrive and the others shared their good news, Thomas said that he would not believe unless he saw the mark of the nails and touched the wound in Jesus's side.

Thomas needed to see and touch for himself. We can be like this too. As babies, toddlers, and young children, we want to taste things, try them out, feel them. There is an air of curious exploration. While doubting Thomas is typically cast in a negative light, I wonder if he didn't also have this sense of curiosity. The death and resurrection of Jesus was so hard for the disciples to understand, even though he had tried to prepare them for it. How could someone who was dead be alive again? How can hope that was so thoroughly squashed be revived? What is this "resurrection"?

Thomas asks to touch—to see and feel—the wounds. Jesus doesn't respond with judgment (which is maybe how we would react). Instead, he says, "Peace be with you." Jesus knows we need to be in contact with his wounds, sometimes with our own wounds too, in order to believe.

For some of us, our wounds are visible. Many of us can point

219

to scars from surgeries, pregnancies, scrapes, and injuries. We remember the story behind those wounds . . . the time we fell off our bike or were in that car accident. We remember how we have been healed.

But we are not the same. We can feel the ridges of that scar, the way it remains present with us. Wounds remind us of past hurt, but they also signal that the wound is not everything. There is healing. There is resurrection.

Consider today that your wounds, even the ones that have caused you so much anxiety and pain, can also be a source of healing and hope, not judgment. Not only that, your wounds can be a way of sharing God's redemptive story with others. We are an Easter people, a people of resurrection. Claim that truth as your own.

Daily Exercise: Wounds Redeemed

Attending to your body is a huge part of your anxiety management plan. This includes activities where you focus on caring for your body, emphasizing healthy habits, and sometimes thinking about changes in these areas. But today, as a way of returning to the body God has given you, just as you are, we offer something of a combination of two activities.

You have become familiar with the body scan activity at this point. Consider combining that activity with a warm bath or shower. Perhaps light a candle as a symbol of God's loving light and gracious warmth being with you. Consider the ways you have sometimes expected Jesus to react with judgment, as you might have with the disciples' fear during the storm and with doubting Thomas in today's reading. Bring to mind this Jesus who does not judge but instead says, "Peace be with you," looking at you with grace and acceptance.

With that same spirit, enter the waters of a bath or shower. Take time to observe your body from toes to fingertips, knowing that all of you is blessed by God. If you run across places that are painful, where there are wounds, remember that God is redeeming those too. Take a breath and remember that Jesus too was wounded and healed, that Jesus brings healing to you and to this world. As you finish your time in the water, remember a prayer of praise and thanks for the gift of your body.

Reflection

We often hear people separate physical health and mental health, our bodies and our minds. But we hope you have heard clearly from us that how we are physically affects us mentally, and our mental state can also dramatically affect our physical body. One only need experience a panic attack to know firsthand how "together" body and mind can be! And it is often in our wounds where we can feel the most broken, physically and mentally.

Today's emphasis on body is not about "fixing" our wounds as much as learning what they can teach us. This is part of the path of redemption and resurrection. As children, we fell down, but we eventually learned to walk.

Consider your wounds today. Where has God provided healing and what may God be leading you toward *through* these wounds? Write about where you may have experienced healing before and where you may see healing beginning now.

_____

_____

_____

_____

_____

_____

_____

_____

_____

_____

DAY 3

MOVING FORWARD

Read Isaiah 40:1–5

A voice cries out: "In the wilderness prepare the way of the LORD, make straight in the desert a highway for our God." (v. 3)

AS WE DISCUSSED EARLIER, ISAIAH foretold the return of God's people from exile in Babylon. It was a word of good news and hope to a people who had suffered much. When I read this passage, I often visualize the highway on which the people traveled through the desert back to their homeland. In my mind, it was a bit of a cartoon affair. A red carpet was rolled out across the sand as people paraded happily through the desert back to a Disneyfied Jerusalem. Bluebirds sang. The sun was shining. All was well.

This was how I visualized this passage until I witnessed the construction that widened a highway near our house. It started with the removal of trees. This alone took months. Next came the moving of power lines and other utilities. It was a year before any asphalt was laid. Prepare the way indeed. Sometimes I hated that road construction. It created hardship and inconveniences for us. There were days when our power was out or a water main burst. It was hard to navigate new traffic patterns. And quite frankly I didn't understand how it was all going to come together to make a better road until the very end. But now I love our new road. It is easier to drive and much safer. Years of hard work and change paid off.

Whether we are talking about laying a physical highway through rough terrain or clearing a path for a journey of healing, a new way requires daily work, effort, and path-building. Some days this will entail the removal of things that hold us back, and some days it will include the construction of healthy pathways we can travel down for years.

The main thing about building this highway is that we have to show up . . . come rain or shine. Whether we feel like it or not, we continue. Whether it is inconvenient or unfamiliar we keep at it. After a while, real progress can be seen. But the daily work can be tedious and boring. Yet each day we are moving forward, a few feet at a time.

To reflect this slow, steady movement toward healing, we will take steps to incorporate physical movement into our lives on a consistent, long-term basis. The movement of our bodies will reflect the movement of our entire selves down the long road to well-being. Though the journey may seem long and sometimes challenging, the destination and even the trip itself will always be worthwhile.

Daily Exercise: Make a Date with Movement

Think back over a movement exercise from the previous weeks (typically day 3) that you have enjoyed. Maybe it was some yoga moves or taking a walk. Maybe your favorite movement activity is something entirely different. It could be ballroom dancing or cycling. Whatever you enjoy that gets your body out and moving, enjoy doing it today. As you practice this movement, think of ways you could make it a part of your regular routine. See if you can make some commitments that will ensure you follow through. Pay for a round of dance classes with your partner, join a running club, buy a six-pack of classes at a yoga studio, or set a weekly time with a friend to walk together. After several weeks of making this enjoyable activity a regular part of your life, you are more likely to keep up the habit of moving your body in healthy and happy ways.

Reflection

When making a plan for movement, we would do well to remember that there are stages of change. Change involves preparation, action, and maintenance. You are being asked to think in a preparation mode again today, planning ahead to take an action and considering beforehand what will be the forces that help you maintain the new behavior. Committing to a class is one way, but committing to a group of others is very helpful too.

Write down what movement you want to incorporate into your day-to-day life. Write down how you will maintain this change (e.g., through a group, through establishing a new habit).

_____

_____

_____

_____

_____

_____

_____

_____

_____

_____

_____

_____

_____

_____

_____

_____

_____

_____

_____

_____

_____

_____

_____

DAY 4

MINDING YOUR THOUGHTS

Read John 20:1–18
Jesus said to her, "Woman, why are you weeping? Whom are you looking for?" (v. 15)

WHEN MARY ARRIVES AT THE tomb and finds it empty, she is confused and sad. She watched Jesus die, so when she sees his empty grave her mind comes up with a scenario that explains his absence. Her mind answers the question of the empty tomb with "they have taken away my Lord" (v. 13). Her thoughts are affected by her grief and beliefs about what is possible.

In the midst of her despair, Jesus comes and speaks life and truth. At first Mary does not recognize Jesus through her tears. She assumes he is the gardener, not her Lord. It is hearing Jesus's voice that clears away her confusion and worry. Recognizing his voice helps Mary understand a new reality. Jesus is not dead, but alive. The empty tomb is not an occasion for tears of sadness but for shouts of joy!

Like Mary, our minds get confused and even warped with untruths and misunderstandings. The distorted lenses through which we view the world lead to false beliefs. You probably have begun to realize this over the past several weeks, but the journey to correct your vision will continue. Your mind will need to be recreated again and again as you connect more fully with the truth.

One step to correct your distorted vision and clear your muddled mind will be to answer a question similar to the one Jesus asked Mary: "Who or what are you looking for?" When you understand the needs and desires of your heart, you will be better able to cast a clear vision for the future.

Maybe you are looking for peace or courage. Maybe you crave

security in the midst of uncertainty. Maybe you are looking for a sense of belonging or belovedness that has been missing from your life. If you know what you are looking for, what scarcity has triggered your fear for so long, you can start to know how to correct your sight.

That day in the garden, Mary was looking for Jesus, her friend and Lord. The ironic thing is that the One she was looking for was already right in front of her. She just had to be able to recognize his presence with her. Maybe as you proceed on your journey through healing, you will recognize places where what you have been looking for has already been with you. Your vision may clear so you can see that what you seek is in front of you. As this happens, may you be able to let the sadness and grief that once defined you make way for new joy and life.

Daily Exercise: Meditation

Find a comfortable position on the floor or in a chair with a posture that is alert but not stiff. Begin to center yourself with the breath and stay with this breath for a few minutes. By now, you may have some experience noticing all the thoughts that are there. When these get distracting, gently return to the breath.

When you feel ready, prayerfully ask the question, "Whom (or what) are you looking for?" Ask this question with the breath. As you breathe and hear the question, let the answers come like drops of rain. When each one falls, receive it without grabbing it or holding it. Let it either run off or sink deep within. See if some part of you recognizes that, even as you ask and answer this question, you already have what you are looking for. See if this becomes clearer as you pray.

"Whom (or what) are you looking for?"

After a few minutes, release the question and come back to your presence in the room and the moment. As you move into the rest of your day and beyond, may you have eyes to see what you are seeking manifest in your life!

Reflection

This is the day of the week when we typically focus on the workings of our thoughts. As we have learned, we are not our thoughts. We can let some of them go; we can hold to others more tightly. As you work through the devotion and daily exercise for today, consider the thoughts you are trying to let go. Write them in the space provided.

Then look for the thoughts you are working to hold on to. Much as the post-resurrection appearances of Jesus announced that something new had happened, look for the thoughts that propel you toward newness of life, toward healing, and toward places where you recognize that God is already with you.

Write these thoughts below.

Old Thoughts

New Thoughts

DAY 5

PLANNING FOR CHANGE

Read Acts 2

All were amazed and perplexed, saying to one another, "What does this mean?" But others sneered and said, "They are filled with new wine." (vv. 12–13)

PENTECOST WAS A PROFOUND CHANGE in the life of the church. Many celebrate this day as the birthday of the Christian church. We return to this passage today in part because of how unbelievable this change appeared to some who only watched the day's events. They thought that those gathered must have been drunk!

Peter seems to be changed in an instant. He went from being a bumbling fisherman to being the lead evangelist of the gospel. Surely the filling of the Spirit of God is a powerful and transformative experience! Although this change seemed quick to those gathered, the change in Peter at this point in his journey had probably been happening over some time. Peter had spent three years by the side of Jesus, hearing him teach, seeing him heal, learning from his ways. Then Peter went through the crucible of his betrayal and Jesus's death, witnessed the resurrection, and then saw Jesus appear again, talking and eating with the disciples.

Maybe the turning point for Peter was not even Pentecost but the moment when Jesus came to him by the sea and asked if he loved him (John 21). After Peter confirmed three times that he loved him, Jesus told Peter to feed his sheep. Maybe the coming of the Holy Spirit was not the moment of change but the moment that Peter was empowered to stand up and be who Jesus had already called him and fashioned him to be, the rock of the church, the shepherd of the people.

Likewise, the change that occurs during our healing from anxiety usually takes place over time. There may be moments when a shift occurs that causes people to look at you twice and wonder who you are or what you have been drinking! However, these big changes will not happen without the small work that occurs daily, weekly, and over time. It is the small, imperceptible changes that add up, allowing you to rise up and become the person God created you to be.

As you go forth from this study, know that your healing will continue with the small work you do every day. Peter had to keep studying, praying, and meeting with people in the name of Jesus in order to be the "rock of the church." He had to keep making adjustments that he did not see coming, such as welcoming the Gentiles or accepting Paul as a partner in shepherding the people.

As your road to anxiety management winds on, changes will continue to manifest themselves. Even as this happens, the road you walk will be made of the small bricks you lay down—doing self-care, keeping boundaries, and staying in community day after day. This will all take time and effort. As with anything, your commitment and your progress will wax and wane, but as long as you keep at it, in the end you will keep moving forward.

Daily Exercise: Making Your Path

Today you are going to plan out your path of continued healing and management of anxiety. Take some time to think about the changes that have been most helpful to you over the past eight weeks. Was it learning to breathe? Starting to move and stretch your body again? Doing work with your relationships? Finding supportive communities to uphold you?

Whatever the good changes were, make plans now that will keep them as part of your life for the near future. Get out your calendar, your cookbooks, your phone, whatever you need to make concrete plans now to make these changes a daily part of life. Maybe you need to block off your lunch hour to walk with a friend, schedule a monthly massage for the next three months, institute a family homecooked dinner night, or just cut off activity early so you can go to bed an hour earlier to practice breathing and meditation before you fall into peaceful sleep. Whatever changes you need, make real time commitments to allow them to be a continuing, habitual part of your life. Better yet, set a check-in night with yourself a month from now to see how things are going and what you need to tweak as you move forward. Find someone in your life (or in the group if you are completing this with others) to hold you accountable for the changes.

Give yourself grace when you get slack and lose momentum. This happens to everyone. The important thing is to keep checking in and keep moving forward day after day.

Reflection

"Wanderer, there is no path, the path is made by walking."[15] This is a quote I have held on to for a long time. I originally discovered it in a book about men by another poet, Robert Bly. The sentiment is the same: "We make the path by walking."[16]

At times this means that we cannot see where we are going until we start moving. For those of us with some fear, that idea alone produces anxiety. Start moving, even without a map for where you are going? But if we do not start moving, taking a few steps in this direction or that, we will not be able to see what is ahead. Maybe we have to go a bit ahead, around a curve, to see the good things that are in store for us!

Hopefully through these weeks, you have made some changes that have led you forward to a different place. Consider where you are now and what you have seen along the way. Think of where you were when you started the study in this book. Write about what you see now that you might not have seen before.

_____

_____

_____

DAY 6

THE PRESENCE OF THE SPIRIT

Read Luke 24:13-35
While they were talking and discussing, Jesus himself
came near and went with them, but their eyes were kept
from recognizing him. (vv. 15–16)

WE DO NOT ALWAYS FEEL God's presence with us. This is one of
the more difficult aspects of the walk of faith. Unlike the sense of
being led to cool waters by the Good Shepherd (Ps. 23), we sometimes feel that we are walking all alone.

I can only imagine that following Jesus's death and resurrection, there were still some dry, lonely times for the disciples. They
were still struggling to understand what it all meant. They had
watched Jesus die a horrible death. While some of them had seen
Jesus since the resurrection, there were many that were relying on
the word of others.

We too may feel some doubt or worry about what others have
said. Like Thomas, we may feel the need to touch for ourselves.

As we return to this passage about the walk to Emmaus today,
notice that the disciples did not recognize Jesus's presence with
them. As they were walking, this "other" person joined them.
They journeyed together, talking and walking for some time, discussing the life and death of Jesus. It was only after they arrived
at the city and were having supper together that they recognized
their walking partner as Jesus. The holy moment of breaking
bread together allowed them to see what had been before their
eyes for some time. Jesus was with them and had been with them.
He was alive and in their midst.

So it goes with us as well. Even though we know Jesus said, "I am with you always" (Matt. 28:30), we do not always see him in our life or feel his presence. We do not always hear his words echoing in our ears. In part, this is because we do not have the gift of Christ embodied among us as the disciples did. Yet we know that through the Spirit Christ is present with us.

As we continue on our walk of faith, what would it mean to be on the lookout for Christ's presence in our midst? We would probably want to be open to seeing Christ even in the unexpected places, not just in our churches or other holy places. Being on the lookout for Christ also involves making time for God to be recognized in our lives. The disciples on the way to Emmaus made the move to invite their walking partner to stay with them for the evening. It was only by inviting him into their space that night that they recognized him as their Lord.

Brother Lawrence, a seventeenth-century monk, talked and wrote about what he called "practicing the presence of God." He made space even in his mundane tasks to praise God and sense God's presence with him. We may not all sense Jesus through washing the dishes like Brother Lawrence did, but maybe we can develop space in our days and weeks so we can recognize God's presence in our lives. In so doing, we may find holy moments during our evening walks, playdates with grandchildren, and coffee dates with friends. The truth of our faith is that Christ is present with us, recognized or not. May we develop eyes and hearts that learn to see him in our midst!

Daily Exercise: Soul Tending

Today you will carve out time to allow your soul to connect with God. Although you can never force God to manifest himself, you will create space for this opportunity to occur. Pick an activity that slows you down and helps you tune into life around you. We find it often helps to get outside in nature, but do what is best for you. If you enjoy gardening, then take some time to garden. Take a walk or sit on a porch and just be. Make space for Jesus to come alongside you and make himself known to you in some way. As you make this space, adopt an attitude of being on the lookout, of watching. Again, no one can force a connection with God, but we can be watchful and wait for Christ to be made known. Maybe you will be touched by the beauty of a flower, the majesty of a thunderstorm, or the laughter of someone nearby. Try not to set unrealistic expectations or get frustrated. Adopt an attitude of restful attention and let yourself be nourished in this time. After twenty minutes, or when you feel finished, let yourself slowly transition back into the rest of your day. Give thanks for any gifts that came through this time. Know that you can continue to carve out soul-tending time as you wish.

Reflection

Where did you find Christ today? Perhaps it was in the daily exercise, or maybe it happened in some other moment during the day. Remember that we are also called to see Christ in others, particularly those who are hurting or lonely (Matt. 25). In this space for reflection today, think of a time when you were surprised by God's presence.

_____

_____

_____

_____

_____

_____

_____

_____

_____

_____

_____

_____

_____

DAY 7

SENT OUT TO COMMUNITY

Read Matthew 10:5–14

As you go, proclaim the good news, "The kingdom of heaven has come near." (v. 7)

WE HOPE THAT ONE OF the truths you have come to realize over the past several weeks is that you have a story to share, a story that is part of the larger story of the gospel, the good news. You have had difficulties that you have weathered. There are lessons you have learned from tough experiences. We trust that you have learned many helpful things as you have read and journeyed through these days and weeks.

As you go forth, we hope you can find pride in your own story. We know there is often a stigma associated with suffering from anxiety, but we believe that anxiety sufferers have no cause for shame. Most likely you have faced dark days and endured. You have not shrunk back from hardships but have learned to persist and overcome. You are a survivor.

With this is mind, we hope that as you move forward you will feel empowered to share the good news. In some ways you are like the disciples in Matthew 10. You have spent time learning and growing, coming closer to God and learning of the healing powers of Jesus. Now you are sent out to live in your community. As you live there, you can connect with others who are hurting and share that good news. You are commissioned as a "wounded healer."[17]

This does not mean you have to share your story with everyone you meet, but we hope you will find appropriate times and places to share your story with those you will meet on the road. Allow yourself to share the bond that comes through struggle. Allow others to walk with you and you with them. Trust yourself to encourage and share wisdom with others.

It can be hard to go forward with confidence and tell the story on your own. You may feel that you are not good enough to share the good news. Or, more simply, that you are not enough. One part of today's passage that has always fascinated Jason is what the disciples were told *not* to take. They were told to take no gold or silver or bags or even extra clothing. There are many ways of interpreting this passage, but one consideration is that the disciples themselves were all that was needed for the task. After all the time they had spent with Jesus, what they had learned from him and experienced with him was enough.

They were enough.

As hard as it is to believe, we are also enough. We are perfectly good vessels for God to use as is.

This does not mean that things will go perfectly. The thing that fascinates Dena most about this passage is that Jesus tells the disciples to "shake off the dust from [their] feet" when things don't go well. Jesus knew there would be days when things didn't go well! The disciples were not expected to achieve perfection. They would have bad days. They would fail.

We will too. When this happens, we are to shake it off and keep going. Trying will inevitably involve some failure, but this does not mean *we* are a failure. We are still loved children of God who get the chance to share the good news as best we can.

Another comforting thought is that we are never alone. God is with us. And we have the support of those who have journeyed with us along the way.

When Dena went through her yoga teacher training, she spent eight weekends with a group of people learning to share their yoga practice with others. At the end of that time, she was quite intimidated to take all the knowledge she had been given and share it with others. She felt intimidated and afraid that she would be alone when she tried to show others what she had learned. This was especially true since much of her learning was a group experience.

Wisely, her teachers gave each student a candle and a blessing at the end of the training as a gift of encouragement. When Dena walked into the yoga room at the YMCA to teach her first class, she took that candle with her to help light the dimmed room. Once the candle was lit and she turned to her breath, she realized she was not alone after all. She had the memories and voices of her teachers and classmates right there in the room with her. To this day when she teaches a certain pose or gives a certain instruction, she can remember the teacher or classmate who shared that wisdom with her.

The truth is that we do not journey alone, but we have a great cloud of teachers and friends who help us along the way . . . even in their absence. When we feel inadequate and afraid, we can remember them and what we learned along the way. Though the disciples were separated from one another, they were together in spirit. Like them we have so many brothers and sisters in Christ on a similar journey. And we always have the Holy Spirit to comfort us.

As you go forth, know we pray for you, and know there is a great cloud of people who are cheering you on your way.

Daily Exercise: Burning the Candle (at One End)

Pick a candle for yourself to be a reminder of being sent forth.

Take some time today to prayerfully light and burn your candle. As you see the light of the candle shine, know the light of Christ is with you. Even if you did not read this book with a group, there are others who support you and others unknown to you who are friends and fellow travelers. Offer a prayer for their journey as they will be praying for yours.

Return to focus on the lighted candle and on the presence of Jesus with you, always and everywhere you go. Take a few minutes to share your worries, fears, and struggles with God as the candle burns. Let them melt away like the wax over the course of your sharing.

When you are ready to blow out the candle, release your worries and let them rise up to God with the smoke. As you prepare to reenter the routine of your day, know that you are never alone in your journey. Know you may relight the candle anytime you need to be reminded of this comforting truth.

Christ has told us, "I am with you always." Amen.

Reflection

Who in your life has shared a story that was good news to your ears? Maybe this is someone who supported you during difficult days of anxiety or someone who shared other parts of their faith story with you. Name those people now.

_____

_____

_____

_____

_____

_____

Who is currently walking the road with you? Who is in your community of mutual support? Maybe these people are friends who also struggle with anxiety or maybe they are folks who feel free to share other life struggles with you even as they support you in return. Plan how you will continue to be in community with these "soul friends."

_____

_____

_____

_____

_____

_____

Who might need a word of good news from you? Maybe this is someone who is new to the journey of anxiety management or someone who is having a hard time and needs some kindness. Plan how you can reach out in love to this person.

_____

_____

_____

_____

_____

_____

In all this remember that as much as we feel God's presence with us in the care we may receive from others, we are also called to be Christ's hands and feet in the world.

CHAPTER 8 REVIEW

There are many places in this chapter where we return to an exercise or thought but with a different approach or perspective. What struck you as new about some of the places where a passage or exercise was revisited?

Are there places where you continue to feel some fear about your journey?

What places are you excited to move toward?

Where do you see Jesus's loving and accepting presence in your life?

There will still be times when you are overwhelmed by churning waters and chaotic waves. When this happens, who are some of the people or what are some of the resources that you can reach for?

Endings and beginnings work together. As you finish this part of your journey, you may find that you encounter some new ways forward too. New paths may have opened to you. New journey partners may have been discovered too! While we celebrate one primary resurrection, we remember that all of us experience many "deaths" and "resurrections" along the way. Our hope is that the process of this book has given you new life in managing your anxiety!

ACKNOWLEDGMENTS

WHILE WRITING THIS BOOK, WE have often recalled the European folktale about making stone soup. We provided a container and some water, but so many people added wonderful and nutritious ingredients to make a delicious soup. Thank you so much to those who have been a part of making this soup! Numerous people have been a part of this journey with us, supporting us, teaching us.

We especially want to thank the first few classes in which we developed and presented this material. You were patient with us and taught us a lot about what would work best for individuals and groups that may travel this path together.

■ ■ ■

I (Dena) would like to thank all my yoga teachers and my yoga teacher-training group. You all taught me so much about breath and movement and about how to be a calm presence for others.

We would also like to thank all the churches we have either served or attended and clergy friends we have made along the way. You have taught us more than we could have expected to learn about the love and grace of Jesus and how to live in authentic Christian community.

They say if you want to be a writer, the best thing you can do is surround yourself with other writers. In that vein, thank you to all my writer friends, especially Word Weavers Macon-Bibb, Word Weavers Page 24, and the crew at Write Brilliant (especially Margaret and Jonathan). You not only helped me believe in myself but also helped me sharpen my craft enough to make this book a reality.

Before I was a writer, I was a reader. So special thanks to my Wednesday Book Group for helping me stay in love with the written word.

As we write in the book, community is key. Thank you to the community of Bare Bulb Coffee that cheered us on as we wrote the first drafts of this book and provided us a space to teach our test-run classes. Also thanks for being amazing people who love on us more than we deserve.

In writing this book I realized how much help I had recovering from my own anxiety disorder. So thank you to all the therapists I have had over the years, my psychiatrists, and all those who made sure I got the help I needed when I needed it. A special thank-you to Dr. Ham and Dr. Richard for being primary care doctors who understand mental health. You never made me feel "crazy" and always guided me with kindness and compassion to seek more help when it was needed.

Thank you to Fay, Steve, and Oliver at Greenbough House of Prayer for providing a shelter in the storm for twenty years. Y'all's love, encouragement, and witness have been a true harbor for our whole family.

Thank you to Diana Flegel and Hartline Literary Agency. Your belief in us as authors and your work on our behalf is greatly appreciated.

Thank you to Kregel Publications, especially Joel, Catherine, Wendy, and Sarah. We are so grateful you took a risk on first-time authors. You not only have made this a better book, but you made bringing this book to life a joy.

Thank you to our friends and family who love us whether we write helpful books or not. Your constant presence and support in our lives means more than you know.

Thank you a hundred times to our children. We know having a mom and dad who write books is not always fun. We are grateful you continue to put up with us anyway. You two are the great joys of our life, and we love you more than you could ever know.

To Jason, my partner in writing and life. Thank you for standing by me and loving me through all my ups and downs. Five years ago on a particularly hard anxiety day, I looked at you and said I wanted to write a book for better dealing with anxiety. Thank you for looking me in the eye and saying, "I will write it with you." This book, much like me, is so much better because of you.

■ ■ ■

I (Jason) would like to acknowledge all that I have learned from my clients who have shared their journeys with anxiety with me. There is a lot that one can learn from education and from ongoing research, but the nuances of lived experience remain our best instruction. It remains an honor to be present with you on your journeys.

In addition to all the multitude of stone-soup "ingredients" that Dena has listed above—to Dena, your willingness to be open-hearted through all of this is a gift to others, but also a gift to me.

APPENDIX
LIST OF RESOURCES

Bourne, Edmund J. *The Anxiety and Phobia Workbook.* 7th ed. Oakland, CA: New Harbinger, 2020.

Brown, Brené. *The Gifts of Imperfection: Let Go of Who You Think You're Supposed to Be and Embrace Who You Are.* Center City, MN: Hazelden, 2010.

Cloud, Henry, and John Townsend. *Boundaries: When to Say Yes, How to Say No to Take Control of Your Life.* Grand Rapids: Zondervan, 1992.

Keating, Thomas. *Open Mind, Open Heart.* 20th anniversary ed. New York: Continuum, 2006.

MacBeth, Sybil. *Praying in Color: Drawing a New Path to God.* Brewster, MA: Paraclete, 2007.

Neal, Susan. *Yoga for Beginners: 60 Basic Yoga Poses for Flexibility, Stress Relief, and Inner Peace.* Pensacola, FL: Christian Yoga, LLC, 2016.

Williams, Mark, and Danny Penman. *Mindfulness: An Eight-Week Plan for Finding Peace in a Frantic World.* New York: Rodale, 2011.

NOTES

1. Susan Neal, "Should Christians Practice Yoga?," Godsgreenery .com, February 27, 2020, https://godsgreenery.com/health -beauty/should-christians-perform-yoga/.
2. Steven J. Petruzzello et al., "A Meta-Analysis on the Anxiety-Reducing Effects of Acute and Chronic Exercise: Outcomes and Mechanisms," *Sports Medicine* 11, no. 3 (March 1991): 143–82. See also Felipe B. Schuch et al., "Physical Activity Protects from Incident Anxiety: A Meta-Analysis of Prospective Cohort Studies," *Depression and Anxiety* 36, no. 9 (June 2019): 846–58.
3. David Eagleman, *Incognito: The Secret Lives of the Brain* (New York: Pantheon, 2011).
4. Contraindications for lowering your head below your heart are uncontrolled high blood pressure, glaucoma, and sinus congestion/bad head colds.
5. Fritz Strack, Leonard L. Martin, and Sabine Stepper, "Inhibiting and Facilitating Conditions of the Human Smile: A Nonobtrusive Test of the Facial Feedback Hypothesis," *Journal of Personality and Social Psychology* 54, no. 5 (1998): 768–77. https://doi.org/10.1037/0022-3514.54.5.768.
6. John Wesley, "I Felt My Heart Strangely Warmed," *Journal of John Wesley*, Christian Classics Ethereal Library, accessed

January 10, 2020, https://www.ccel.org/ccel/wesley/journal.vi .ii.xvi.html.

7. Katherine Harmon, "How Important Is Physical Contact with Your Infant?," *Scientific American*, May 6, 2010, https://www .scientificamerican.com/article/infant-touch/. See also Maia Szalavitz, "Touching Empathy," *Psychology Today*, March 1, 2010, https://www.psychologytoday.com/us/blog/born-love/20 1003/touching-empathy.

8. Karen B. London, "Oxytocin: Chemistry Between People and Dogs Is Real," *Bark*, February 2019, https://thebark.com/con tent/oxytocin-chemistry-between-people-and-dogs-real. See also Maria Petersson et al., "Oxytocin and Cortisol Levels in Dog Owners and Their Dogs Are Associated with Behavioral Patterns: An Exploratory Study," *Frontiers in Psychology* 8 (October 2017): 1–8.

9. A wonderfully helpful resource on this topic is Bessel van der Kolk's *The Body Keeps the Score: Brain, Mind, and Body in the Healing of Trauma* (New York: Penguin, 2015).

10. Contraindications for lowering your head below your heart are uncontrolled high blood pressure, glaucoma, and sinus congestion/bad head colds.

11. Barbara Brown Taylor, "As a Hen Gathers Her Brood," *Christian Century*, February 25, 1986, 201.

12. James O. Prochaska, John C. Norcross, and Carlo C. DiClemente, *Changing for Good: A Revolutionary Six-Stage Program for Overcoming Bad Habits and Moving Your Life Positively Forward* (New York: HarperCollins, 2006).

13. Christopher R. Pryce and Adriano Fontana, "Depression in Autoimmune Diseases," *Current Topics in Behavioral Neurosciences* 31 (2017): 139–54. See also George M. Slavich and Michael R. Irwin, "From Stress to Inflammation and Major Depressive Disorder: A Social Signal Transduction Theory of Depression," *Psychological Bulletin* 140, no. 3 (May 2014): 774–815.

14. British Psychological Society, "Why Singing in a Choir Is Good for You," ScienceDaily, December 4, 2013, https://www.science daily.com/releases/2013/12/131204202705.htm.

15. Antonio Machado, "Proverbios y cantares XXIX," in *Selected Poems of Antonio Machado*, trans. Betty Jean Craige (Baton Rouge: Louisiana State University Press, 1979).

16. Robert Bly, *Iron John: A Book About Men* (Boston: Da Capo, 2015).

17. See Henri J. M. Nouwen, *The Wounded Healer: Ministry in Contemporary Society* (London: Darton, Longman & Todd, 1994).

ABOUT THE AUTHORS

JASON HOBBS, LCSW, MDIV, IS a licensed clinical social worker in an outpatient mental health clinic. He has been in private practice for more than fifteen years in addition to having worked in hospice and homeless services in Richmond, Virginia, and Savannah, Georgia. While in Savannah, Jason also pastored a small United Methodist congregation for three years. He has led multiple workshops and retreats on mindfulness-based cognitive therapy and spiritually sensitive clinical practice, in addition to the interaction between religion, spirituality, and health. Most recently he completed a course leading to a certificate as a spiritual director through the Shalem Institute.

DENA HOBBS, MDIV, IS A campus minister to Episcopal and Lutheran students. She has previously served as a United Methodist pastor, a stay-at-home mom, and a teacher of Christian yoga. Dena has journeyed through anxiety and panic disorder for twenty years and finds great meaning in helping others manage and heal their anxiety. Dena enjoys leading workshops and retreats on Christian spirituality, especially family spirituality, the liturgical church year, and contemplative practices. She previously self-published *Lighten the Darkness*, an advent devotional. She lives in Middle Georgia with Jason, their two teenagers, and two hound dogs.